FOLLOW FIRST, LEAD SECOND - LEADERSHIP IS FOR EVERYONE!

TABLE OF CONTENT

A SUMMARY OF LEADERSHIP 3
INTRODUCTIONS 4
LEADERSHIP 5
WHAT ARE THE QUALITIES THAT DISTINGUISH A GREAT MANAGER? 9
THE CHARACTERISTICS OF A SUCCESSFUL LEADER 11
LEADERSHIP'S SIGNIFICANCE 13
LEADERSHIP THAT WORKS 14
WHAT'S THE POINT OF HAVING A LEADER? 14
AS A LEADER, WHAT IS YOUR ROLE? 16
WAYS TO IMPROVE YOUR LEADERSHIP CAPABILITIES 17
RELATIONSHIP AND DISPARITIES BETWEEN LEADERSHIP AND MANAGEMENT 19
LEADERSHIP VS. COMMAND AND CONTROL 22
5 WAYS TO IMPROVE AS A LEADER 25
LEADERSHIP SKILLS IN THE WORKPLACE 28
A NEW GENERATION OF YOUTH LEADERS 30
WHY IS A LEADER IMPORTANT? 34
HOW TO BECOME A MORE EFFECTIVE ORGANIZATIONAL LEADER 39
TRAINING FOR THE LEADERSHIP DEVELOPMENT PROGRAM 41
THEORIES OF LEADERSHIP IN THE BUSINESS ENVIRONMENT 44
THE SITUATIONAL LEADERSHIP THEORY IS THE THIRD TYPE OF LEADERSHIP THEORY. 47
WHAT EXACTLY IS THE TRAIT APPROACH? 55
FACTORS THAT INFLUENCE THE EFFECTIVENESS OF AN ORGANIZATION'S BEHAVIOR 60
HOW DO CHARISMATIC LEADERSHIP AND SUBORDINATE PERFORMANCE INTERACT? 67

A SUMMARY OF LEADERSHIP

ABSTRACT:
There is the widespread belief that management and leadership are inextricably linked, that every manager is (or should be) a good leader. As a result, management leadership has been elevated to a cause worthy of promotion, and leadership as a term has become a mantra chanted by all and sundry, with numerous voices proclaiming numerous theories, many of which are spoken as facts, particularly by those who are disciples of this management-leadership cause. Examples of their output can be found in any management texts, in texts specializing in engineering management, and, as one might expect, in texts devoted exclusively to the leading cause. Numerous literary fallacies and paradoxes will be examined, and an unusual literary source will be used to illustrate various leadership styles.

The concept of leadership will be applied to engineer positions, and some potentially divisive conclusions will be presented.

Leadership is a critical field because it affects the entire world. In other words, it is a vital management function that enables organizations to achieve maximum efficiency and effectiveness. Numerous individuals inquire why we should pursue this field of study or why this assignment is necessary. Not only is leadership a position, but it is also a process that shapes how people and organizations interact. All nations, business enterprises, educational institutions, and organizations succeed primarily due to effective leadership.

INTRODUCTIONS

There are many different connotations associated with the term "leadership." For example, a political leader is devoted to a personal cause, such as that of a politician.
For an explorer, clearing the path through the jungle so that the rest of his team can follow, or for an executive, developing the company's strategy to outperform the competition.

Leaders' help others follow their example and do the right thing. Set a course and build a vision that inspires others. For a team or an organization to "win," leadership necessitates a dynamic and exciting period of action.

To get their people to the right place, leaders must use management skills to help them get there smoothly and efficiently.
The subject of leadership will be the primary Focus of this book. We'll focus on Bernard Bass's "transformational leadership" model, first put forth by James MacGregor Burns. In contrast to management processes designed to maintain and steadily improve current performance, this model emphasizes visionary thinking and a desire to bring about change.

NOTE:
People around the world and in different situations see leadership in various ways. For instance, it could apply to community, religious, political, and campaigning group leadership.
The task of identifying and defining 21st-century leaders is a unique one. Organizations, individuals, and influencers are all attempting to reshape the notion of leadership as a new skill set. A taxonomy that makes sense of today's problems and endures beyond the time of its creator is being fought over by everyone in the industry.
When it comes to leadership, these are the fundamentals:
Considerable effort has been made to redefine leadership for the twenty-first century.

THE FOLLOWING ARE SOME OF THE INITIATIVES AND THEMES:

- Self-awareness and self-control
- There is a lack of leadership morality, innovation, and risk-taking and the presence of gurus like Jack Welch and Rudy Giuliani.
- A new global definition of leadership
- Leadership as a career – an additional competency for some organizations,
- An embodiment of all competencies for others

LEADERSHIP

WHAT QUALITIES MAKE A PERSON A LEADER?

Effective leadership is critical to any structured organization's long-term success. Executive leaders are responsible for setting and achieving goals as they determine and guide an organization's direction and purpose. Others, some of whom may lack the title of leader, are critical to the success of a business. We'll define leadership in this article and discuss how to develop into a successful leader.

SO, WHO EXACTLY ARE THE PEOPLE IN CHARGE HERE?

While the title of the C-suite executive is often used to describe someone's position as a leader, leadership is more about a person's attitude and behavior.
In the past, we've all seen examples of top-tier managers who do helpful work efficiently but fail to lead in any meaningful way. They keep things running smoothly, but they don't inspire or motivate. At the same time, lower-level employees may inspire and mobilize their coworkers to achieve the company's goals. 83 per cent of organizations agree that developing leaders at all levels is critical to the company's success.

Organizational leaders can set themselves apart from community leaders and politicians by focusing on their company's goals at all times. Effective management in the workplace isn't some esoteric concept. If an organization does well in employee engagement, productivity, and profit, people will ultimately judge leadership.

As we'll see, leadership isn't a one-size-fits-all endeavor. Depending on the circumstances, what works for one organization and one situation may not apply to another. Effective leadership is critical regardless of the size or scope of a company, and without it, things will quickly come to a crashing halt. Because of this, every company should have a clear definition of what good leadership means to them.

WHEN YOU'RE IN CHARGE, WHAT DOES IT MEAN TO LEAD?

To be a leader, you must motivate and direct others to achieve a specific goal. To accomplish one's goals, one's job as a leader is to encourage others to take action. Acquiring and honing the necessary skills is essential to becoming a great leader. Fortunately, anyone who is willing to put in the time and effort will develop these skills.

From CEOs and senior executives to supervisors and project managers, leaders can be found at every company level. Even as an entry-level employee, you can put your leadership abilities to use by training new employees or leading a meeting. Depending on the team and the situation, each leader may have a distinct leadership style or a combination of several. In addition, there are a variety of leadership styles, such as:

- **GOAL-ORIENTED:** Sets predetermined rewards for achieving them
- Focuses on setting and accomplishing company **OBJECTIVES.**
- **AUTOCRATIC:** Prioritizes efficiency in setting goals.
- Listens and incorporates team member's ideas in a **DEMOCRATIC** manner

Individuals, projects, and businesses can all benefit from various leadership styles.

THE 13 CHARACTERISTICS OF AUTHENTIC LEADERSHIP, COMPARED TO REGULAR MANAGEMENT, ARE:

1. In the battle between government and innovation,
2. Original versus copy
3. Maintaining rather than developing Focus on systems
4. Structures vs. a people-centered approach
5. Acceptance vs. investigation:
6. Control vs. inspiration Perspectives:
7. Short-term vs. long-term
8. Comparing interest in "what" vs. "how" vs. "when"
9. Imitation versus originality:
10. A focus on the bottom line versus a long-term goal
11. Assumption rather than opposition to the status
12. Quo Individuality versus conformity
13. A person's desire to do things correct versus their ability to do so

TRANSFORMATIONAL LEADERSHIP QUALITIES INCLUDE:

Consistency and clarity are essential to building trust in an organization, which is why a clear vision is so necessary for the organization's future. By focusing on their strengths, people can demonstrate a positive view of themselves.

❖ **WHAT DOES IT MEAN TO BE A TRANSFORMATIVE LEADER?**

Since James V. Downton coined the term "transformational leadership" in 1973, it has remained the most common leadership style. People are drawn to charismatic leaders who genuinely care about the well-being of the people they work with. They usually have a high level of emotional intelligence and are always looking for ways to improve themselves and those around them through their actions and responses. For them, project management is all about delegating authority and responsibility to their team leaders and letting those leaders handle the day-to-day details. Because it aligns so well with contemporary ideas about what constitutes excellent leadership, this is a valuable asset for companies hoping to attract top-tier employees.

Despite his reputation as an inspiring and visionary leader, Steve Jobs has also been accused of being manipulative and humiliating his employees, more in keeping with the traits of an autocrat. Despite this, he took great care in setting up the Pixar offices so that employees could share ideas and build on each other's work. There were only two toilets for all employees to use, so they had to walk a long distance away from their workstations and bump into other people on the way. Edwin Catmull, the CTO, convinced him to install a second set of toilets.

❖ **IN WHAT WAYS DOES TRANSACTIONAL LEADERSHIP DIFFER FROM OTHER FORMS OF LEADERSHIP?**

The goal of a transactional leader is to unite the team around a common objective that everyone on the team can work toward and achieve. When goals aren't met, there are consequences and interventions to deal with the failure to meet those goals. When it comes to their employees, transactional leaders are careless. They don't put much emphasis on building relationships with them or learning about their concerns on a personal or professional level.

Goal-oriented leadership can feel cold, but it often follows Maslow's Theory of Hierarchical needs in order to create a strong sense of employee satisfaction when the team accomplishes its objectives.

In his early years, Bill Gates was considered a transactional leader before becoming a transformational leader. When Bill and Melinda Gates started their foundation, they had no idea what they were getting themselves into, but now they are the world's largest philanthropic organization. In his role as a manager at Microsoft, he was meticulous about following the proper chain of command and stayed laser-focused on getting things done. For this reason, transactional leaders tend to be excellent at achieving short-term goals, but less so at communicating long-term vision.

❖ WHAT KIND OF LEADERSHIP IS AUTOCRATIC?

Being seen as authoritarian and dictatorial, autocratic rule seems to be the least relevant leadership style today. In some cases, such as when decisions must be made quickly due to time constraints, it can be beneficial.

Autocratic leaders adhere to rules and prefer to work in environments that are highly structured and rigid. Their management style discourages team members from taking initiative, allowing them to make their own decisions, or cultivating creativity. The day-to-day management of the business and the day-to-day decision-making of the leadership teams are entrusted to them. Even in today's workplace, the style is outdated, but unfortunately, it persists in less forward-thinking companies.

WHAT DOES IT MEAN TO BE A THOUGHT LEADER?

Think leadership isn't about how you lead, but rather how much you know about leading. Blogging is one way to do this, as is writing white papers and using social media sites like Facebook and Twitter.

Although it can be powerful in finding an organization's target audience, a strong leader's opinion on current events may be polarizing if not everyone agrees with it. A leader who speaks his mind, like Elon Musk, attracts followers who can identify with his ideas, even if they worry about what he will say next. Patagonia (led by Yvon Chouinard) is a great example of a company with a strong purpose or values that can be used to speak out on issues like sustainability and diversity.

WHAT ARE THE QUALITIES THAT DISTINGUISH A GREAT MANAGER?

Misconceptions abound about what makes a great leader and what qualifies as having excellent potential for leadership. There is no one-size-fits-all job description for a successful leader because each person's leadership style is unique. Great leaders are aware of their weaknesses as well as their strengths and are always open to new ideas.

The University of Lincoln's MSc management program can help you discover and develop your leadership skills while also exposing you to the most current management best practices.

WHAT IS THE PROCESS OF LEADERSHIP?

Any definition of leadership in business must take this into consideration, because in business, leadership is directly linked to results. As a result, even though leadership isn't always linked to financial success, those who are seen as effective leaders in the business world are also those who see their company's profits rise.
Leadership positions can be terminated if they fail to generate profits as expected by board members and executives, as well as by shareholders and investors.
It's possible for anyone to develop the leadership qualities they lack, even if they appear to be born with more of them than others. Leaders who have risen to the fore in times of crisis despite having no prior leadership experience abound throughout history. They were able to assume leadership roles because they had the right traits and qualities.

ADVANTAGES OF HAVING A STRONG SENSE OF DIRECTION

Among the many advantages of developing one's leadership abilities are the following:

KNOWING YOUR STRENGTHS AND WEAKNESSES IS SECOND NATURE TO YOU.

It's important to know your strengths and weaknesses as a leader so that you and those under your leadership can see your full potential. As the manager of a team, project, meeting, or other entity, you will quickly discover your strengths and weaknesses because they are often magnified and reflected by the group.

YOU'LL HAVE A BETTER SENSE OF THE DIRECTION THE BUSINESS IS TAKING.

Understanding your company's objectives is critical as your role as a leader develops. A better understanding of your employer's point of view is essential to succeeding at work. It will also help you and your team set clear objectives.
Your team's motivation can be boosted by providing them with incentives.
In order to motivate your team, you may want to learn more about how to be an effective leader. This may help you discover the best ways to do so. Increasing the productivity and morale of your team can help you meet your goals more quickly if you have the right kind of motivation in place.

YOU HAVE THE POWER TO UNITE YOUR GROUP.

An effective leader must have a clearly defined goal or vision. Your team's path to success can be clearly defined if you know what you want to accomplish. Teamwork is easier when everyone understands their roles and the goals you have set for them.
You'll be able to keep more members of your team.
They can accomplish more and have a greater sense of pride in their work when you know how to lead your team effectively. When your team members feel like they've accomplished something, it's easier for them to stick with you and the company as a whole.

THE CHARACTERISTICS OF A SUCCESSFUL LEADER

Many soft skills are required to be an effective leader. If you want to succeed as a manager, you must have strong technical skills that are relevant to the team and the industry in which you work, in addition to those of yourself. Many soft skills are required to be an effective leader. If you want to succeed as a manager, you must have strong technical skills that are relevant to the team and the industry in which you work, in addition to those of yourself. In your quest to become a better leader, keep the following tips in mind:

FLEXIBILITY

As a leader, you'll come into contact with a wide range of individuals, systems, and activities. These aspects are subject to frequent modification. Knowing when to be flexible will help streamline processes and encourage members to grow and learn new skills. Take, for instance, someone on your team who is particularly good at a new task. Consider giving them additional tasks that will allow them to build on this new skill rather than requiring them to finish their original project.

EMPATHY

In order to better understand others, build trust, and cultivate friendships, you must practice empathy. You should be available to listen to their successes and challenges, and if necessary, provide advice and guidance. The more you know about your team's actions, the more efficient your work processes will be.

DECISIVENESS

When you're in charge, you'll have to make tough choices all the time. You have to be able to make a decision quickly and rationally at times. Analytical tools like data and SWOT analyses can help you make better decisions. Taking the time to think about your past decisions and the decisions of others will help you make better ones in the future.

COMMUNICATION

Talking can ease tensions and boost productivity. It can also improve communication among members of your team. Open communication with your team and explain any changes that occur as you work toward your goal are essential to a successful project. The ability to actively listen to the needs and an idea of those around you is another important aspect of effective communication. In order to ensure that your team understands exactly what you want and what you expect from them, be as specific as possible in your communication.

TIPS ON HOW TO BE A BETTER MANAGER

To become a great leader, one must put in the time and effort. Some people spend the majority of their professional lives trying to figure out what it takes to be an effective leader. Start by taking the following steps in order to develop basic leadership skills and hone your own management style.

1. FIND A MENTOR.

A mentor can assist you in identifying the most effective leadership techniques for you. Together, you can determine your most valuable assets and how to best utilize them. Additionally, they can assist you in developing goals to strengthen areas of weakness. Finding a mentor can be as straightforward as asking around at work, contacting old contacts, or utilizing your professional network.

2. CONDUCT INDEPENDENT RESEARCH.

If you want to improve your leadership abilities, there are many resources available to you, including books, articles, and podcasts. Studying the skills of people who inspire you is also a good way to learn how they achieve their goals.

3. PUT IT INTO ACTION.

If you want to maintain your leadership qualities, you must practice them. In order to improve your craft, keeping a journal of your practice sessions is a valuable tool.

4. ENROLL IN A COURSE OF STUDY.

There is a wide range of leadership training courses available, both online and in-person, including group seminars and one-on-one sessions. Consider taking a leadership training course if you want to learn more about effective leadership practices and how to implement them. Find out if your company has any programs to help you grow as a leader.

5. IDENTIFY YOUR OWN LEADERSHIP STYLE

Identifying the best leadership style for you, your team, and your organization can be helpful. As the demands of their team shift, most leaders employ a hybrid approach.

6. ASKING FOR FEEDBACK

In the same way that individual contributors should receive regular feedback about their performance, you can ask your team for constructive feedback to help you improve. What worked for them and what didn't should be able to be identified and improved upon by your team. As a result, you'll be in a better position to lead.

LEADERSHIP'S SIGNIFICANCE

To succeed, you must have good leadership, says Taillard. "With good leadership, you can create a vision and can motivate people to realize it." Every employee in an organization can be motivated to do their best work by a good leader's example. In other words, to be effective, leadership must draw in, motivate, and keep as many people as possible.

In order to improve efficiency and achieve objectives, leadership is an essential management function. Leaders, who have a clear vision, motivate their employees, and guide the organization toward its goals are effective. Any position can benefit from a better understanding of leadership roles in order to make a more meaningful contribution to the achievement of the company's goals.

In this book, we focus on the importance of leadership and how it affects an organization's fortunes.

WHAT IS THE SIGNIFICANCE OF BEING A GOOD LEADER?

Leadership serves a number of critical roles in an organization's success. A leader's primary responsibility is to set the company's direction. It is the leader's job to convey the organization's mission and its goals to its members.

Even though an organization may include people with a wide range of skills and talents, it is the leadership that brings them together to accomplish the overall goal. Leaders' help their companies excel by inspiring and motivating their teams and coordinating their individual actions in support of a common goal.

WHAT IS THE PURPOSE OF HAVING A LEADER IN A GROUP?

The best teams are made up of a diverse group of individuals, each of whom brings a unique set of strengths and abilities to the table. However, the majority of organizations still prefer to have a team leader in order to better direct the energy of their members. In order to be successful, your group will require the guidance of a strong leader.

LEADERSHIP THAT WORKS

As a general rule, people are drawn to follow a guiding figure. A higher level of authority can help you achieve more, regardless of your level of expertise and experience in a given field. That's because a good leader gives you direction and works with you to minimize the risks that could harm your output. Mentorship, accountability, and delegating responsibilities are all ways in which a leader can improve your chances of success even if they aren't senior colleagues.

Leaders with a clearer understanding of the team's purpose and what it must do to achieve that purpose have a better chance of succeeding. In order to inspire others to work with them in order to achieve their goals, leaders must be able to guide as well as understand and communicate the organization's vision. It is the leader's responsibility to make sure that everyone on the team knows what their responsibilities are and to create an environment that encourages them to do their best work.

VALUES SHOULD BE PROMOTED.

Leaders can inspire others to adopt essential values that are critical to the success of the organization. Your team members will follow your example if you are honest, trustworthy, on time, and a good role model. Employees and clients alike will benefit from a culture of accountability and taking responsibility when things go awry.

ENHANCE INVENTIVENESS.

A company's creative climate can be enhanced by the leadership of team members. Providing employees with more freedom in how they carry out their duties is a great way for leaders to help others see the bigger picture of the company. Improved efficiency and productivity can be achieved by gaining new insights into how tasks should be carried out and decisions made.

WHAT'S THE POINT OF HAVING A LEADER?

An organization's long-term strategy and goals can only be achieved with the help of a strong leader who provides direction, purpose, and clarity. Here are 11 reasons why effective leadership is worth the price of admission:

1. PERCEPTION

To be successful, leaders must have the ability to communicate their vision for the organization's future. In order to get their company where it wants to go, leaders lay out a strategy that outlines the steps and resources needed to get there.

2. AFFECTIVE EXCHANGES

It's the job of leaders to help employees understand the company's vision and mission. In this way, everyone is able to identify the roles that best suit their abilities and experience. Leaders encourage their subordinates to take action in order to achieve their goals through clear communication.

3. MAKING A CHOICE

Effective decision-making is a hallmark of effective leadership. In every situation, a successful leader makes the best decision for the organization. The ability to make sound decisions under pressure is a hallmark of effective leaders. They take into account their organization's strengths and weaknesses to ensure that the decisions they make now and in the future are in the best interest of their company.

4. AROUSAL OF EMOTIONS

Leaders have a burning desire to accomplish their goals, and they radiate that enthusiasm to those around them. Leaders who are effective inspire others to support the company's goals and give everyone a compelling reason for continuing to work hard.

5. ASSISTING

Effective leaders supervise their employees' work to ensure that they perform their roles effectively. Workers are more productive when their efforts are coordinated with organizational goals, which is something leaders strive to achieve.

6. COMMITMENT

An effective leader is devoted to the well-being of their company and its people. They don't let short-term setbacks dampen their spirits and focus on the company's long-term goals. Motivation and encouragement from leaders help their teams overcome obstacles and get back on track when things go awry.

7. AUTHENTICITY

Ethical values can only be taught to an organization by a leader who is successful. If you want to succeed as a leader, you must do the right things, no matter what obstacles you face. Integrity, honesty, and fairness are all important values to them, and they expect them from their company and the people who work for it.

8. CONFIDENCE

Confidence in one's subordinates' abilities is one of the most powerful leadership tools. They are there to listen to their employees' concerns about their work, to give them constructive criticism, and to make sure the office environment encourages their best work.

9. INSIGHT

Trusting a leader can improve employee morale. In doing so, it communicates to workers the leader's faith in their ability to carry out the company's vision and mission. As a result of a positive work environment, employees are more likely to focus on the company's objectives.

10. GROWTH

To be an effective leader, you must create an environment where your subordinates are able to learn and grow. They are open-minded and eager to learn from the successes and failures of others. It has been observed that leaders who get the most out of their employees' suggestions for how to improve the company's efficiency and innovation do so by rewarding their workers for their efforts.

11. ASSEMBLING A TEAM

A good leader is one who is able to strike a balance between their own goals and those of the company. Leaders are aware that their employees work for their company for a variety of reasons. They foster an atmosphere in which the company's objectives can be met without compromising the well-being of its employees.

AS A LEADER, WHAT IS YOUR ROLE?

THE FOLLOWING ARE THE PRIMARY RESPONSIBILITIES OF A LEADER:

Leadership is essential at every level of management.
Collaboration in the formulation of strategies and policies is critical at the highest echelons. It is necessary for the interpretation and implementation of top-level plans and programs at the middle and lower levels. When plans are put into action, leadership can be demonstrated through the guidance and counseling of subordinates.

When it comes to an organization's representative, it's typically a manager or leader. He has to speak on behalf of the issue at conferences, seminars, and other gatherings. He is tasked with articulating the business's rationale to the general public. In addition, he serves as a spokesperson for the division in which he serves as the head.

Personal and organizational goals are integrated and reconciled. A leader's leadership traits help to reconcile and integrate the personal goals of employees with the objectives of the organization. Achieves goals by coordinating the efforts of various people toward a common goal. This is only possible if he has the ability to influence and elicit cooperation and a strong desire to achieve the goals.

He enlists the help of subordinates. A leader is also a manager who enlists the help and cooperation of subordinates. It's possible for him to do so because of his unique combination of personality traits, intelligence, maturity, and experience. In this regard, a leader must solicit ideas and, if possible, incorporate them into the company's plans and programs. If he can gain the full support of his employees, the company's operations will run much more smoothly.

The qualities of a mentor, a friend, and a philosopher are all necessary for a leader. Sharing his thoughts, feelings, and desires with his coworkers can make him a better friend. When the time is right, he can act as a philosopher by drawing on his knowledge and experience to offer guidance to the company's workers. He can serve as a guide by ensuring that top management's plans and policies are communicated to the company's employees and by ensuring their cooperation in achieving the company's goals. As a counselor, he can offer advice and help people come up with solutions to their problems. He has the ability to listen to the concerns of his employees and work toward a solution.

WAYS TO IMPROVE YOUR LEADERSHIP CAPABILITIES

The good news is that you can improve your leadership skills even if you don't hold a management position right now.

BUILD UP YOUR SELF-DISCIPLINE
For both managers and their subordinates, a strong sense of discipline is essential. Discipline can be improved in a variety of ways, including by meeting deadlines, staying on top of work responsibilities, and showing up on time for work.

TAKE ON ADDITIONAL DUTIES
To be a leader, you must take personal responsibility for your actions as well as those of those around you. It's a good idea to ask for more responsibilities at work in order to prepare yourself for the increased sense of responsibility you will feel as a leader. As a result, you can show your employers that you are capable of taking on additional responsibilities, which will help you land a promotion in the future.

LEARN TO PAY ATTENTION.
Taking the time to hear what other people have to say can help you learn new skills and improve your working environment. In order to be an effective leader, one must be willing to accept criticism, suggestions, and feedback from their team members. Learning from mistakes helps them move forward.

CREATE A SENSE OF URGENCY
To become a good leader, you must begin to see the big picture. Think about the possible issues that could arise in various situations, and devise ways to deal with them if they do.

MOTIVATE OTHERS
Encourage and motivate your coworkers to achieve their goals. This could be accomplished by praising them for their efforts and providing them with encouragement and guidance as needed.

DON'T GIVE UP ON EDUCATION!
Learn as much as you can to be ready for anything that may come your way in the future.

BE A SOURCE OF INSPIRATION FOR OTHERS
Delegate some of your work to your coworkers. It's not only beneficial to delegate tasks to experts, but it also relieves some of the burden from your shoulders.

SOLVE ISSUES THAT ARISE
Leaders must keep in mind that their team members will not always get along. Be ready to talk to your team members privately if you need to help them solve their issues. Also, if the conflict cannot be resolved, consider reassigning team members to other roles.

DON'T ABANDON YOUR EDUCATION!
Learn as much as you can to be prepared for whatever comes your way in the future.

DISCOVER WHAT DRIVES YOU.
You must be enthused about what you do in order to be successful in your leadership role. Make an effort to find a job that aligns with your interests. Even if you're not sure what your true passion is, this worksheet can help you discover it.

CREATE AN ONLINE PERSONA THAT IS DISTINCT FROM THE ONE YOU'VE BUILT UP AT WORK.

Consider joining a non-profit organization or a sports team if your current employment does not allow you to assume leadership roles. You'll be able to work with others more effectively and hone your leadership skills if you follow these measures.

PAY ATTENTION TO THE TEAMS YOU'RE A PART OF.

Observing other people's behavior is a great way to pick up a lot of useful skills. If you're a member of a group, pay attention to how the group's leader acts. Try to learn from their mistakes so that you don't make the same ones yourself in the future.

RELATIONSHIP AND DISPARITIES BETWEEN LEADERSHIP AND MANAGEMENT

A large number of people believe that leadership and management are interchangeable terms. In order to be a successful manager, you must recognize that leadership is an essential element. For a manager to be effective, he or she must exhibit excellent leadership behavior by fostering an environment in which every employee may grow and flourish. According to one definition of leadership, it is the ability to influence and encourage a group of individuals toward achieving a common objective. For example, promotion to higher levels of management within an organization can be a formal source of influence in the workplace.

In order to be an effective manager, he or she must have the qualities of a leader. Leaders devise and implement strategies that help them gain and maintain a competitive edge. It is imperative that organizations have leaders and managers who are capable of leading and managing effectively.

LEADERSHIP VS. MANAGEMENT: THE DIFFERENCES

When a manager sets the framework and delegated authority and responsibility, a leader provides direction by developing the organizational vision, communicating it to employees, and inspiring them to reach their goals.

When it comes to management, planning, organizing, staffing, directing, and controlling all fall under the umbrella of leadership. People follow leaders because they listen and build relationships with them. Leaders also build a team by working together and motivating their subordinates.

- Managers have authority because of their position in the organization, whereas leaders have authority because of their followers.

- Organizational policies and procedures are strictly adhered to by managers, whereas leaders follow their own intuition.

- Science-based management requires managers to be meticulously organized and methodical in their approach to the task at hand. As for leadership, it is a skill that must be learned. It's a given that leaders are needed if managers are to be employed.

- Unlike management, which focuses on an organization's technical aspects or job duties, leadership focuses on the organization's human resources.

- When it comes to evaluating employees, management looks at their names, past records, and current performance; leadership looks at their potential, which can't be measured, and deals with the future and how people will perform if their potential is fully realized.

- Leadership is proactive if management is reactive.

- Managerial communication is based more on written communication, whereas leadership communication is based more on oral communication.

It is impossible for organizations that are over- or under-managed to perform at a high level. Leadership and management work together to create a new course of action and make the most effective use of available resources. As a person and as a business, leadership and management are critical.

MANAGERIAL AND LEADERSHIP ROLES ARE NOT INTERCHANGEABLE TERMS.

Leaders and managers are often viewed as interchangeable terms, but this is not the case. Managers aren't necessary for leaders to be. Management does have a component of leadership, but it is not the primary focus of management. However, the roles are often intertwined and both are critical.

Managers and executives alike make significant contributions to the success of the organization. While managers are more concerned with the broad picture, they are also more concerned with the day-to-day minutiae of how to arrive at their destination. These are the individuals who will be in charge of the company's day-to-day operations and who will assist the organization in achieving its objectives. Leaders, on the other hand, will be burdened with the responsibility of encouraging and influencing others.

Some people think of management as a science, while leadership is a more creative art form. There are many differences between managers and leaders, so let's take a closer look.

A LEADER: is a person who has the authority to make decisions based on his or her personal qualities, and who is focused on the vision of the organization. Mainly concerned with big-picture thinking / innovation.

MANAGERS: based on positional authority; process-oriented; working within an organization; structurally oriented; primarily concerned with the finer points

As a result, the two roles are intertwined. Leadership and management are not mutually exclusive roles; both are necessary for a successful organization. Managers, on the other hand, are responsible for identifying and overcoming any obstacles that the leader may be unaware of or insensitive to.

Some of the characteristics of leadership are necessary for managers to succeed, in order to at least persuade others to support their vision. However, while it is common to find leaders at the highest levels of an organization, this does not mean that they are necessarily involved in management.

LEADERSHIP VS. COMMAND AND CONTROL

Having legal power is necessary for exercising authority, and people are willing to obey those who hold it, regardless of their personal characteristics or political position in the organization. Leaders in organizations and other settings, regardless of whether they occupy formal positions of authority, rely on the informal power they possess over others in order to exercise their influence. They are respected and trusted for their judgment, not just because they hold a certain position in the organization. As an example, Mahatma Gandhi was not in charge of the Indian independence movement for the majority of his life.

When faced with adversity and crisis, people tend to see authority and power as an oppressive force that must be resisted. This makes it difficult to achieve the desired results. Leadership, on the other hand, tends to attract followers through the exercise of free will and choice rather than coercion. The people over whom authority is exercised rarely have the opportunity to provide feedback, criticism, or opinions, but leaders give their followers ample opportunity to do so.

Only relying on authority when dealing with adults doesn't work, but leadership provides a better approach of sharing and involving thus building rapports and creating long-term relationships. A leader inspires his or her followers through self-modeled ways, and thus leadership has a greater impact on people's attitudes and behaviors than authority can.

While exercising authority restricts people's ability to think creatively and come up with novel solutions to issues and problems, leadership fosters an environment where people are encouraged to look beyond the obvious and think outside the box.

According to Stephen R Covey, one of the most significant differences is that leaders have moral authority over their followers, which is absent in the case of power from authority. Leaders who have moral authority on their subordinates by establishing asynchrony in their words and actions in the organizational setup create a robust and transparent culture in the workplace.

Rather than collaborating with other functions and departments as is necessary, leaders today often work in silos rather than cooperating across functions and departments. It's tough for managers and leaders to communicate outside of their small circle of influence. Leadership and management, however, are more effective when leaders step out of their comfort zone and assume overall responsibility for the entire organization.

Later generations will continue to use and benefit from the ideologies and thoughts of individuals like you who don't rely on authority but instead lead by example. Individuals in positions of authority are remembered and followed because they were the ones who actually led their people.

MOTIVATION AND LEADERSHIP

People who are self-motivated are more likely to achieve their goals. An individual is compelled to work harder to achieve his or her goals as a result of this. In order to influence employee motivation, an executive must possess the appropriate leadership characteristics. Motivation, on the other hand, does not follow a predetermined formula.

To be a good leader, one must maintain an open mind about the nature of people. The decision-making process will be much easier if you are aware of the needs of your subordinates.

Leadership and motivational traits are essential for both the employee and the manager. Effective leadership requires an in-depth understanding of what motivates others. Employees, peers, and bosses all have basic needs that he must be aware of. Leaders use their position to inspire others.

THE FOLLOWING ARE SOME ESSENTIAL GUIDELINES OUTLINING A FUNDAMENTAL VIEWPOINT ON MOTIVATION:

- Assist subordinates in coordinating and aligning their own demands with those of the organization's overall objectives. An executive's responsibility is to make sure that the company's morals and ethics are in accordance with what the organization expects from its personnel. A manager's job is to guarantee that his employees are motivated and educated in a way that is consistent with the needs of the organization.

- Recognition and rewards play a significant role in encouraging people to achieve their goals. A small token of appreciation, such as a certificate or letter, can be a powerful motivator. There must be an explanation of why the recipient of a certificate has been honored in the text.

- For example, being an inspiration and motivator for others can help them achieve their goals. As a leader, you must set an example for your employees so that they can grow and succeed.

- Participation in decision-making processes such as planning and resolving critical issues not only inspires people, but it also educates them about the complexities involved. In addition, everyone will have a clearer idea of what their responsibilities are within the company. In order to get the leader's attention and appreciation, the communication will be clear and concise.

- A company's health is directly correlated to its ability to foster a sense of morale and camaraderie among its employees. The moral fabric of a person is made up of his or her thoughts and feelings. Subordinates' morale can be affected by the actions and decisions of a leader. Because of this, he should be aware of his decisions and activities at all times.. The heart and soul of a company is its team spirit. Always make sure that your subordinates are having fun while working together and are a part of the organization's long-term goals.

- A leader should put himself in the position of his or her employees and see things from their point of view. When things get tough, he should be able to sympathize with them. Their mental and emotional strength grows as a result of you sympathizing with their hardships.

- Employees who complete a meaningful and challenging task feel accomplished. The executive must make their employees feel that their work is critical to the success of the organization. As a result of this motivating factor, they work harder to achieve their objectives.

To be an effective leader, you must be self-motivated. You need to know who you are, what you want, and what you're willing to do to get there. Self-motivation is the only way to inspire others to work toward their own goals and to align their personal objectives with those of the organization as a whole.

WHAT ARE THE KEYS TO EFFECTIVE TEAM LEADERSHIP?

Team leadership can be viewed in a variety of ways. An individual designated leader is the norm in more traditional models. Delegation is a skill that must be mastered by the person in charge of the project. To get the most out of their team, they'll need strong interpersonal skills, such as the ability to praise and criticize in a way that is both constructive and encouraging.

It's time for a new approach to team leadership. An individual team leader is not required in this setup. Instead, team members take on leadership roles as appropriate to the circumstances and the scope of their experience. Thus, there is no set hierarchy, and the performance of every team member contributes to the overall success of the group.

5 WAYS TO IMPROVE AS A LEADER

Leadership isn't always an instinctive thing to do. If you want to be a great leader, you have to keep an eye on your own performance. Here are some tips to help you improve your abilities.

RECOGNIZE YOUR AREAS OF WEAKNESS.

To begin, consider your personal leadership style. 'Do I allow my team members to make their own decisions?' When a company goes bankrupt, how do I handle it? Once you've identified your areas of weakness, you can work on strengthening those areas.

You can help foster an open and honest work environment by soliciting feedback from your employees. Preventing old habits from creeping back into your work is easier if you review your performance on a regular basis.

BE SPECIFIC ABOUT WHAT YOU WANT TO ACHIEVE.

It's impossible to stay on track if you don't have a plan. Think long and short term so that you can maintain momentum, and make sure to include both individual goals as well as company-wide goals.

A time for review is also necessary. As long as the situation is going well, there is no harm in tweaking a goal's scope or setting an example and raising one's own expectations.

YOU NEED TO IMPROVE YOUR ABILITY TO COMMUNICATE EFFECTIVELY

In order for you and your team to succeed, you need to be able to communicate effectively. It all begins with leaders taking the time to listen to and understand their employees' thoughts and feelings. In order to build trust, you'll need to pay attention to what the other person is saying and follow through on any promises you make.

There must be a sense of trust and openness in the workplace. By encouraging your team to get in touch with you in a way that works best for them, you'll keep your visibility high and make it easier for them to get in touch with you.

MAKE SOME MISTAKES AND LEARN FROM THEM.

To be a sound leader, one must be able to identify when something goes wrong and devise a strategy for preventing it from happening again in the future. You may decide to collect input from within your organization or conduct a review of prior decisions in order to discover areas for improvement.

Mistakes can shape a person's character. Make sure you've learned from your blunders and that you have faith in your future decision-making abilities. As a general rule, leaders who are open about their mistakes tend to be more respected than those who try to hide them.

WORK TOGETHER WITH THE PEOPLE ON YOUR TEAM

Leadership doesn't mean doing everything on your own. The best bosses encourage their employees to join them in even the most challenging of endeavors. You'll reap the benefits of a more engaged workforce if you put your trust in your coworkers.

➢ WHAT IS THE SIGNIFICANCE OF LEADERSHIP IN THE FIELD OF BUSINESS?

Whether you're in charge of a non-profit, a government agency, or a for-profit business, you'll need a strategy for the future of your organization. That vision requires leaders who can plan and carry it out effectively.

Whether it's enlisting others' help in completing tasks or figuring out which tasks are most important in the first place, leadership plays an important role in the workplace. Leadership in business administration is critical, and we'll examine this issue in greater detail below.

WHEN IT COMES TO BEING A LEADER IN THE WORKPLACE, WHAT DOES IT MEAN?

How would you define "excellent leadership" then? A difficult question to answer, and one that is also very subjective, can be difficult to answer. There are various ways to be a leader in the workplace. Careers in which leadership is an essential part of the job description can be found. CEOs are the company's top strategists, and they literally serve as the company's leader. However, leadership skills can be used in a wide range of positions throughout an organization, even at the highest levels.

There are several characteristics of a good leader, according to the Center for Creative Leadership, a non-profit organization dedicated to leadership development that has worked with hundreds of Fortune 1000 companies. Learning agility—the ability to learn quickly and apply that knowledge in critical situations—is among these characteristics. Leaders place a high value on the ability to effectively communicate. With the "courage" that comes with leadership, an effective communicator can not only better delegate work amongst the people on their team and communicate information to them clearly, but they can also use their communication skills to bring up new ideas that can boost profits while also shaking up the current order of things.

While the boardroom and the battlefield are vastly different environments, the defining characteristics of leadership are very similar. One of the most distinguishing characteristics of leaders is their ability to take swift action. In battle, a private has a 20% chance of initiating combat, while a senior officer has an almost 70% chance of doing so. In the workplace, it's common to see similar behavior. Taking control of one's life might be difficult. It's considerably more challenging if you're unsure of what needs to be done - if you're unable to perceive the "larger picture.

In the case of corporate trainers, for example, they are responsible for imparting new skills to a wide range of employees, all of whom must have a thorough grasp of the company's ever-changing needs in terms of products and services. Or, to put it another way, an appreciation of the big picture.

It is important for human resources (HR) managers to be involved in strategic planning and to have an understanding of how each employee's unique skills and abilities relate to those of the entire organization. When it comes to leadership, it's like many other business administration careers.

WHAT ARE THE BENEFITS OF HAVING A STRONG LEADER IN THE WORKPLACE?

As the owner of a business, you may have to decide how to delegate responsibilities, deal with interpersonal conflicts, handle unexpected issues, and develop your vision for the company. In order to overcome these kinds of issues, business administration leaders are essential.

In fact, it is impossible to overstate the importance of leadership in business administration. The impact of a leader, good or bad, can be felt throughout an organization at the highest levels. It's a great way to energize your team and give them a sense of direction. An organization's corporate culture and growth trajectory can be influenced by strong leadership. Great business leaders such as Bill Gates, Elon Musk, Steve Jobs or Warren Buffett can be found in both modern and historical contexts.

During his tenure at GE, Jack Welch helped the company grow from a $12 billion valuation to a $505 billion one by acquiring hundreds of companies. As a result of his leadership, the company's operations were changed to force employees to accept change, and he hired managers who he knew could keep employees engaged. Decisions made by the top down can have a significant impact on the origination of a company.

However, leadership can be critical even at lower levels of management and in roles that don't appear to be leadership positions at first glance. It is critical for a corporate leader to inspire and motivate people, to build a sense of shared purpose, to foster a culture of mutual respect, and to provide clarity and direction to the organization. Management, in the words of Steve Jobs, "is about convincing people to do things they don't want to do, whereas leadership is about pushing people to do things that they never thought were possible."

LEADERSHIP SKILLS IN THE WORKPLACE

FOUR OF THE MOST IMPORTANT LEADERSHIP QUALITIES IN THE WORKPLACE ARE:

- People are more likely to follow your lead if they see you living what you preach. If you expect your coworkers to put in their full effort, but then leave early, you could be damaging morale. People are looking for leaders who will answer to them for their actions.

- Writing and vocal communication can play a significant part in leadership, as has been previously noted. It is essential for leaders to be able to put themselves in another person's shoes or to have cognitive empathy so that they can connect with their subordinates.

- Goleman's best-selling book Emotional Intelligence makes a compelling case for the importance of "emotional intelligence," which he refers to as "emotional intelligence." Self-awareness, empathy, motivation, social skills, and self-regulation abilities are all part of it.

- You must be able to see the big picture if you want to be a good leader. A wide spectrum of both hard and soft talents may be required for success. Identifying market shifts and the potential for new items to enter the market could be examples of this.

There is much more to come, however. You'll also need skills like teamwork, problem-solving, motivational, analytical, and conflict-resolution abilities. Inexperienced leaders can enhance their leadership skills by learning how to better listen for input from their team members.

LEADERSHIP STYLES IN THE BUSINESS WORLD

When it comes to leadership in the workplace, there are a variety of styles to choose from. Bureaucratic leadership is counterproductive if you want to foster an environment that encourages innovation and new ideas. The following are four of the most popular designs:

- When it comes to making final decisions, Democratic leaders rely on informal polling to help guide them. Democracy allows leaders to take advantage of the wisdom of their employees more easily than in a more hierarchical setting. Although it can increase employee engagement, this leadership style can slow down decision-making.
- Decisions are made without consulting others, and you, the expert, are in charge. " Quick decision making can benefit from this, as well as the ability to exclude those who aren't qualified. When people feel they aren't involved in important decisions, it can have a negative impact on their confidence in the process.
- In contrast to authoritarian, top-down leadership, servant leadership is characterized by an emphasis on serving others. Serving the needs of their team and creating a positive work environment is the goal of the servant-leader. This model may be slower to solve problems than autocratic leadership when you have to make unpopular choices, but there are scientific links between employee happiness and productivity.
- When it comes to expectations, bureaucratic leadership is all about establishing a set of rules and procedures that everyone must follow. Innovative or creative problem-solving processes do not benefit from this leadership style, but routine-oriented jobs do.

Considering your own strengths and weaknesses is an important consideration when evaluating the various leadership styles. There may be more persuasiveness required for servant leadership than for autocratic leadership. There are many different leadership styles to choose from, and finding one that works best for you can take a combination of education and experience.

A NEW GENERATION OF YOUTH LEADERS

Young people can be leaders when they take charge of their own lives and those of others. Self-awareness and self-determination are two of the most important characteristics of young people who demonstrate leadership in the world today. Every day, young people have the opportunity to lead by example, lead by following, and lead through their own hard work and dedication. Whether it's three people or 3,000,000, youth leadership can include actions that impact other youth, younger children, and adults.

There is a possibility and reality that young people can become powerful, engaged leaders for social change, according to The Freechild Project's belief in youth leadership development.

Non-traditional youth leaders are helping to broaden the scope and depth of youth leadership activities by partnering with young people from all walks of life. This group of young people, who are focused on race and socioeconomic differences, also includes BLGQTT students, low-achievers and dropouts, and youth from alternative family backgrounds.

Instead of simply leading in a vacuum, today's youth leaders learn, explore, and examine as much as possible about their communities, families, and society in order to become more effective, engaging leaders. As a result, they are making a difference by taking action that has a visible, observable effect.

Accepting the status quo and perpetuating dull adult perspectives on youth isn't enough for many youth leaders today, nor is critical thinking and critical action. From the perspective of social justice, they are adopting radical new approaches to change the organizations, communities, and societies in which they have been entrusted as leaders.

Tools Youth Leadership Education is the Only Way to Make a Difference in the World. Youth leaders must be given the opportunity to learn about the world in a real and meaningful way through practical action. Reflection, critical thinking, and cultural actions are excellent ways to demonstrate that you've learned about the issues we've discussed on this site....

The fun and games begin when a neighborhood, organization or society refuses to change. Achieving tangible results in one's own or another's life or the lives of others is possible when young people and adults work together.

There is no need for youth to rely on adults to create opportunities for youth leadership. But when they form youth/adult partnerships, they have a better chance of making a difference

ARE THERE ANY SYMBOLS OF LEADERSHIP THAT ARE POSITIVE?

For the most part, traditional leadership archetypes are based on the concepts of power and authority. Workplace relationships can be portrayed as a dynamic between a commander and his troops using military imagery. It is said that lions and kings rule because of their high social status, which can be attained through noble birth or extraordinary talent. It is also possible to use leadership symbols that speak more to the power of working together rather than to individual egos.

THE WAITER OR WAITRESS

Innocent says that the symbol of the servant leader represents a powerful transformation in which the leader plays a supporting role rather than being at the forefront of the organization. An overly prescriptive manager may be able to get things done, but he or she will not be able to empower his or her employees to make their own decisions and act responsibly and creatively. The opposite is true for a servant leader, who empowers his or her employees by instilling in them self-awareness and a sense of purpose. This low-key approach boosts morale and motivation, encourages new ideas, and helps to keep employees engaged and educated.

Few leaders step into fully formed businesses and run them in accordance with predetermined systems.

THE BUILDER.

Businesses often start out small and require on-going upkeep and repair in order to remain operational. According to the Harvard Business Review, leaders who work as builders bring humility to the process of running their organizations and are willing to get down to the nitty gritty of solving problems. On a foundation of successes and failures, the structure can be improved.

INSIGHTS FROM THE TRAINER

Sportsmanship in the workplace encourages teamwork while enhancing the abilities of workers individually and collectively. When it comes to coaching, it's the coach's job to help each member of the team shine. According to the Globe and Mail, successful coaches, like successful managers, have a deep understanding of each employee's talents and weaknesses. Individual strengths and traits can be tapped into in the right situations, allowing team members to grow and develop new skills and abilities.

By harnessing the unique skills and personalities of its employees, Artist Leadership aims to create something more than the sum of its parts. A successful leader, like an artist, has a vision. If you communicate effectively and collaborate with your coworkers, you will be able to explain this viewpoint to them. As an artist makes sense of a landscape, they connect seemingly disparate sections and present these connections in unique and clear ways.

SIMPLE EXERCISES IN LEADERSHIP

You can use leadership games to improve teamwork and communication while also developing leadership skills in those who participate. Additionally, they can be used to assess the leadership potential of a group in a non-threatening environment. There are many more complex ways to test and strengthen leaders, but starting out with simple tasks is often the most beneficial.

LEADERSHIP EXERCISES BASED ON A SPECIFIC PLAN

In an envelope, put a set of blueprints and blocks on the table. Decide who will be the group's leader and let them vote on it. The blueprints for what they're going to build can only be viewed by this person. They can't say what the group is trying to build or touch the blocks; they must guide the team to follow blueprints and build what they've drawn. If you're working with a large group, consider setting up several tables, each with a different set of people, and having them rotate to a new table when they finish their task.

Setting out a jigsaw puzzle, blindfolding the team except the leader, and then guiding them to complete it without touching any of the pieces themselves is an alternative method.

A STORY THAT IS TOLD ONE SENTENCE AT A TIME

Ask the group to tell a story, and have each member contribute a sentence. In addition to being an excellent team-building activity, this is an excellent leadership exercise because it requires participants to think creatively, plan ahead, and adapt as the situation changes, all of which are essential skills for leaders. If you look closely, you'll see that those in the group who are truly in charge try to add a sentence that aids those who will follow them, rather than veering the narrative off course.

TOSS THE BASKETBALL

With their hands clasped, the group stands in a circle, with one member of the group swaying a hula hoops. To complete the challenge, each team member should pass the hula hoop around the circle without breaking their own arm until it reaches the original person's arm and is returned to them. In order to effectively communicate with one another on both a physical and verbal level, this is an excellent game for honing teamwork and communication skills. Hula hoops can be passed more efficiently when one person takes on the role of a "leader" in this game.

THE MINEFIELD CAN BE NAVIGATED

The first step is to divide the group into two equal groups. Each pair must then have one of their members blindfolded, as in the alternative version of the blueprint leadership game. Then a minefield of cones, balls, and papers is constructed around them. As the leader of each pair, the blindfolded partner must be guided through the obstacle course using only a few preselected words, such as "forward," "back," "left," and "right." Team members who touch an obstacle with the blindfolded person are disqualified. The team that completes their course in the shortest amount of time wins.

LEADERSHIP STYLES THAT ARE DIFFERENT

You should use this game to teach new employees how to be good leaders or to improve the leadership skills of a group of existing managers. Set up four-person teams for everyone. Three people will pretend to be the fourth person's superiors. It is expected that each of the leaders will be assigned one of three leadership styles: bossy, aggressive, or passive. It then comes to light that they have to confront their employee with a problem, such as tardiness, cutting corners, or a bad attitude toward customers and coworkers. Afterward, the group should gather to discuss how the boss could have handled the situation more effectively..

WHY IS A LEADER IMPORTANT?

A positive corporate culture is the result of the hard work and dedication of a company's leaders. Good leadership, on the other hand, is a learned skill. Personal traits such as integrity, dedication, vision, a sense of fairness, and creativity are all characteristics of good leaders. By listening well and motivating others, good leaders inspire the best in others. Despite the fact that some leadership qualities are innate, others can be learned.

HOW TO TELL IF A LEADER IS A GOOD ONE

The term "leader" refers to someone who exerts influence over a large group. Anyone who has the power to influence their coworkers' thoughts and feelings, as well as their beliefs and actions, can be considered a powerful person. A title isn't necessary for a person to be considered a leader. Leaders are judged by the impact they have on others.

PERSONAL CHARACTERISTICS OF A SUCCESSFUL MANAGER

According to Michelle C. Bligh in "Personality Theories of Leadership," there are five major leadership qualities: conscientiousness, agreeableness, neuroticism, openness, and extroversion. Researchers have found that a good leader is intelligent and self-confident; he or she is sociable; and they have a high degree of integrity.

THEY ARE ABLE TO CONNECT WITH OTHERS

Listening, motivating, delegating, and providing long-term visions are some of the qualities of a good leader. Practice and education can help leaders become better listeners. A leader inspires her subordinates to work hard, and she motivates them to do their best work. Leaders must have a clear and comprehensive vision, as well as the ability to delegate delicate tasks.

AN EFFECTIVE LEADER IS CONSTANTLY EXPANDING THEIR KNOWLEDGE BASE.

Leaders may be born with the ability to influence others, but the best leaders never stop learning. Leaders, who participate in accountability groups, attend leadership conferences, and read books on leadership development are more likely to succeed. An article published on SelfGrowth.com by Bob Pearce, entitled "Leadership—What Makes a Good Leader," outlines the characteristics of a good leader.

Those in positions of authority who are capable of seeking feedback do so.

A professional leadership consultant's assessment can help a leader improve his or her leadership abilities. A leader's strengths and weaknesses are discovered through this type of consultation, and an action plan is developed to address both personal and professional needs.

WHO, WHAT, AND HOW TO BE A SUCCESSFUL LEADER

There must be leaders who can guide and persuade others toward a common objective. An effective leader is one who can inspire others to trust in his abilities and vision. Leaders with traits like these are more likely to be trusted, respected, and promoted into positions of authority because of their strong morals, beliefs, intellect, and extraversion. The term "born leaders" is used to describe these leaders. It's not uncommon for most leaders to go to school in order to better themselves so that they can help others succeed. They are known as "process leaders" because of their constant involvement in educational activities aimed at inspiring others and helping them achieve their goals. Anyone can learn how to be a good leader.

Make a name for yourself in your field by becoming an expert. Without the ability to perform well, you will have a hard time convincing others to put their faith in you as their leader. Learn everything you can about your job by taking classes and reading up on everything you need to know. You'll gain the respect of your followers if you do this.

Your vision should be conveyed. Your followers will have a better understanding of what they need to do if you give them a clear picture of what you want them to accomplish. Explain how each employee contributes to the company's overall success.

Observe human behavior and address the needs of each individual. Leaders have a genuine concern for the people they are in charge of. There is no one-size-fits-all approach when it comes to managing people. For example, one employee may be highly motivated but lacking in technical expertise. One of your coworkers may be extremely competent in the realm of technology, but he or she has trouble meeting deadlines. Determine the best way to help each individual succeed by assessing their needs.

Develop virtues such as honesty, fairness, and a willingness to help others, as well as a strong work ethic and the ability to think creatively.

Decide wisely in a short period of time. Complete projects on time and keep the company moving forward by using problem-solving skills and assessments. Weekly or biweekly meetings are the greatest approaches to keep your team informed about the status of your initiatives.

Give others a voice and a chance to make a positive impact on the company's growth. To be a good leader is to create an environment where others can grow and contribute.

Both Trait and Skill Approaches to Leadership Define Key Personality Traits and Link the Traits to Successful Leaders. Self-assurance, intelligence, sociability, and tenacity are a few of these qualities. Leaders are born, not made; some characteristics are more suited to leadership than others, and those who rise to the top have the proper combination of characteristics. According to the skill approach, leadership is regarded as a skill that can be learnt and refined over time. Educational opportunities can help you develop technical, interpersonal, and conceptual talents, all of which are considered essential leadership characteristics.

SUBJECTIVITY

Assessing who is a good or successful leader is difficult because what one group considers success may differ significantly from what another group considers success. As a result of this focus, the skills approach places greater emphasis on the successful training of leaders and the means of enhancing the leader's performance.

INCONSISTENCY

According to the traits theory of leadership, successful sales managers are optimistic, enthusiastic, and dominant, while production managers are more introverted, cooperative, and respectful of others. However, the skills approach believes that leadership skills can be learned and developed, and therefore, any manager has the ability to learn the skills that are required in his or her field of work.

CHARACTERISTICS OF THE BODY

Weight, height, and other physical attributes, as well as one's overall health and well-being, are all part of the traits model. In spite of the fact that these traits may have some correlation with other factors, they have no bearing on performance at all. For effective leaders, the skills approach model doesn't consider physical attributes to be a necessary precondition.

INFLUENCE

The ability to persuade others is a crucial component in all of these professions. In a nutshell, an effective leader is able to persuade others to do what they want them to do. A person is a leader within an organizational framework that includes a structure, various cultures and subcultures, individuals, and groups of individuals. Organizational goals are achieved through a leader's ability to motivate others to carry out a set of tasks in support of those goals.

FOCUSED ON THE LEADER

Both strategies put the focus solely on the leader, with no thought given to the followers or the organization's relationship to them. They believe that leadership is largely a function of one's personal qualities. In order to be an effective leader, one must have certain inherent abilities in addition to the ability to learn on the job.

LEADERSHIP STYLES THAT INSPIRE CHANGE

There are many management models today, but transformational leadership is one of the most popular. It is based on Max Weber's 1948 research, which Sir McGregor Burns expanded on in the 1970s, which found a link between charisma and leadership. There are four main concepts or styles that make up the model, which are sometimes called the "four I's": idealized influence, inspirational motivation, individual consideration, and intellectual stimulation.

INFLUENCE IN AN IDEALIZED STATE

Being a role model is the most basic form of idealized influence. Leaders who are able to transform organizations do so by modeling the behaviors they want to see in their teams. Maximilian Weber's original research on charismatic heroes influenced idealized influence. When people look at history's most successful leaders, they see people who are the best at what they do and aspire to be like them. In the workplace, transformational leaders put this philosophy into effect.

MOTIVATION THAT IS BOTH INSPIRING AND MOTIVATING

Inspirational inspiration necessitates a shared vision for the organization's future that everyone shares. Transformational leaders motivate their teams to work harder and smarter in order to achieve the organization's vision. In order to achieve success in this dimension, one must have a specific amount of charisma in order to convert influence into action. Leaders foster a culture of teamwork that motivates employees to take action in order to achieve the bigger company's mission and strategic goals. Inspirational motivation, on the other hand, motivates employees to take genuine action in order to make the vision a reality, whereas idealized influence promotes a vision and demonstrates the proper way to behave.

INDIVIDUALIZED CARE AND ATTENTION

Every organization, whether expressly transformational or not, uses some type of customized consideration to teach or strengthen the abilities necessary for success in one way or another. Individualized consideration can take the form of coaching, mentoring, and advising, among other things. Transformational leadership requires leaders to identify and meet the needs of their employees in order to improve the broader organization. The goal is to identify and transform the important abilities that employees posses into assets that will aid in the realization of the organization's vision. It demands a fundamental grasp of the requirements and motivations of employees.

STIMULATION OF THE INTELLECT

Intellectual stimulation acknowledges that long-term success is unattainable without the ability to think creatively and innovatively. Transformational leaders foster the development of new ideas and the application of innovative ways to current organizational problems. It is encouraged rather than condemned when people challenge long-held beliefs. Managers help to stimulate intellectual stimulation by continually demanding higher performance and better results from their employees. Employees in an ideal organization, one that gives all of the resources necessary to meet these difficulties, respond with inventive ideas that help the organization exceed expectations and outperform its competitors, according to the firm's vision.

HOW TO BECOME A MORE EFFECTIVE ORGANIZATIONAL LEADER

Organizational change management must be managed consistently and effectively by those in charge of leading the organization. If management is unable to quickly adjust to changing circumstances and drive the company in the appropriate direction, an organization will suffer from a lack of appropriate leadership.

Companies at various phases of development require a variety of different types of leaders. It follows that organizations are more effective when leadership procedures are entrenched throughout the company, allowing different people to take on leadership positions at various stages throughout the organization's lifecycle. In a layered organization, the leaders in each tier rely on one another for their success. It is possible to increase productivity within an organization by boosting the quality of its leadership.

Improve the flow of information from the top down. Any changes in the company's direction should be communicated as soon as possible and at all levels of the organization.

Create a mission statement for your organization and make sure that all of your activities are in line with that mission statement. Example: If your company's major objective is to develop premium skincare products for ladies over 50, all marketing and promotion efforts as well as all research and development efforts should be directed toward anti-aging skin care for women over 50.

Create task groups that bring together senior leaders from across the organization to debate strategy and implementation. Instruct the task forces to collaborate in order to develop short- and long-term road maps for the organization that are consistent with the organization's vision.

Create a compensation system that relates employee bonuses to the performance of the individual, the team, the division, and the company.

Formalize an organizational hierarchy chart in which people's authority is assigned based on their existing position in the company. Allowing people to take on greater responsibility and change roles as they progress through their careers will help them to become more effective leaders.

HOW TO EVALUATE LEADERSHIP CAPABILITIES

The most effective way to inspire people is to lead by example, and behavior takes precedence over abilities first and foremost when it comes to leadership. Human attributes such as attitudes and behaviors, as well as abilities that go beyond conventional conceptions of authority, are necessary for effective leadership. Having a clear vision and keeping the big picture in mind at all times is vital for a strong leader to be successful. A good leader is capable of giving commands, evaluating performance, resolving problems, and setting the tone for the organization. Followers are naturally drawn to leaders that inspire others, demonstrate integrity, and can build confidence in their followers that they will do what is right in every situation.

Take a look at the job description. Investigate the position's duties and responsibilities, as well as the areas of leadership that have been recognized.

Inquire with the individual about what she perceives to be her own personal strengths. Inquire as to which areas she would like to see improved in her performance. Take notes during the meeting so that you may refer back to them later.

Carry out a 360-degree evaluation. Create an evaluation instrument that evaluates motivational skills, personal factors, organizational aptitude, and technical talents, among other things. Include everyone in the process of evaluating the person's leadership abilities, including supervisors, subordinates, back-office workers, and clients.

Review all of the data that has been collected at the same moment. This will give you a general idea of the person's leadership style and characteristics. If some of the evaluations were done on a scale of 1 to 5, make the necessary computations.

Concentrate on behaviors that can be observed. Choose specific instances of intelligence, self-confidence, integrity, sociability, and determination from the 360-degree assessments to share with the class or group.

Examine how successfully the individual motivates and encourages team members to participate. A good leader would encourage and assist others when they are in the limelight, understanding that their success is a reflection on him. He will also encourage his employees to be innovative and to take some risks in their work.

Decide whether or not you will require the individual to participate in an in-person or online leadership evaluation. Compare and contrast the data with the feedback you've heard from others to have a better sense of how to assess the person's leadership capabilities.

CREATING GOALS AND OBJECTIVES FOR EMPLOYEES: A GUIDE

To effectively manage your workforce, each member of your team must understand what is expected of them and be motivated by the problems that they face on a daily basis. As a manager, your success is dependent on your ability to successfully coach your team through the formulation of performance and skill development targets. Effective goals and objectives serve as the gasoline that propels the growth of your company and its personnel to greater heights.

Take into consideration the company's goal and mission. Determine what each employee can bring to the table that will help the organization achieve its mission. Make use of the abilities of your team to develop goals that take advantage of each employee's unique strengths in order to move the company closer to achieving its vision.

Make a list of the precise responsibilities that each employee must complete in order to be successful. Specific goals direct your employees' efforts toward the things that are most important to your company. Time management and resource allocation become more efficient when goals are established in advance. Provide explicit examples of the outcomes you anticipate each employee to achieve.

Create each objective in such a way that you can receive feedback on a consistent basis. When you read the goal, you and your partner should both understand how you will determine if he is on pace to fulfill the objectives you have set for him.

Establish completion dates for each target. Your employees will appreciate the structure and clarity that time constraints bring. Deadlines discourage procrastination and encourage your team to be more productive with their time.

Review your goals and objectives with each member of your team on a regular basis. Maintain an open mind to the inquiries and concerns of your employees. They may be in need of resources that you can supply or information that they can gain through training, which you can provide. As a team, you may provide answers to their queries, provide what they require, and motivate them to work at a high level through regular meetings to discuss progress.

TRAINING FOR THE LEADERSHIP DEVELOPMENT PROGRAM

In the words of ManagementHelp.org, "leadership development is an activity (ideally planned in nature) that improves the learner's ability to lead oneself as well as other people, groups, and organizations." People in leadership roles receive training in leadership development programs that offers them with the inspiration, direction, and tools they need to effectively lead themselves and others. As a result of the program's training, highly driven, capable leaders who are proactive and imaginative in their leadership abilities should emerge.

PURPOSE

In order to do this, leadership development program training should clearly describe the leader's tasks and competencies, as well as her action plan for achieving her objectives. The goal is to educate executives on how to be more successful change agents and on how to apply effective management concepts to their organizations. Its goal is to teach leaders how to guide themselves via their own personal and professional development processes.

When it comes to training leaders, a leadership development program may take a number of different techniques. Team-building activities and leadership principles are frequently used in training programs to demonstrate team-building and leadership principles through hands-on experiences. For example, a leadership training program may require participants to participate in a sports event in order to teach ideas of cooperation, organizational communication, and the importance of leadership. Other methods of training may include group discussions, lectures, reading leadership literature, and participation in accountability groups, among others.

IMPLEMENTATION

When leaders complete a leadership development program, they should always be provided with an action plan that they can utilize to put the new knowledge into practice when they return to their previous positions. The leaders may be requested to put down their interpersonal communication strengths and limitations, for example, if the training was focused on successful interpersonal communication. The leaders should put a phrase or two next to each weakness detailing how they intend to improve that particular shortcoming. They will be able to actively concentrate on improving those areas when they return to their jobs.

OUTCOME

Effective leadership development programs will produce leaders who have excellent people skills, a clear sense of direction, and the capacity to communicate effectively both interpersonally and across the organization as a whole, among other things. These leadership characteristics will have an impact on those underneath the leader, providing them with a higher sense of purpose, job satisfaction, and direction in their work. This will result in a solid internal structure for the firm as well as a positive corporate culture for all employees. It also builds trustworthiness in the leadership's relationship with their subordinates.

CONSIDERATIONS

Leadership development is not something that can be done in a single day, but rather is a continuous process in which the leader accepts personal responsibility for educating, inspiring, and being proactive in his or her own self-improvement and training. Taking part in leadership conferences, reading books on leadership skills, and soliciting input from colleagues are all effective ways to achieve this goal.

THE DIFFERENT TYPES OF LEADERSHIP IN AN ORGANIZATION

Companies may need to appoint successful leaders in order to remain competitive in the business world. Leadership styles have an impact on how employees see their positions in the organization, and this can have an impact on their overall productivity. Because no two businesses are alike, leaders may be chosen based on the specific corporate culture (values, beliefs, and conduct) or if the major focus is on productivity or establishing connections among people. Hiring highly qualified executives who are a good fit for the organization may be important to a company's long-term success.

THE AUTOCRATIC LEADER IS A PERSON WHO HAS ABSOLUTE POWER.

The autocratic (also known as authoritarian) leader has complete authority to make choices and tell subordinates what they should do in order to achieve his or her goals. With this style of management, employees may have limited opportunities to share their thoughts or comments. This form of motivation can be based on fear, such as threats of job loss, or it can be based on employees' allegiance to a specific leader. This style is quite dominant, and it discourages independent thinking and originality. It might be most effective in a circumstance where production is of the utmost importance.

THE DEMOCRATIC PARTY'S CHIEF EXECUTIVE

Subordinates are solicited for opinion and assistance in decision-making by the democratic leader (also known as participative leader or participative management). Democratic leaders may be able to recognize and capitalize on the abilities and skills of their employees for the benefit of the organization. This technique may be more popular among employees who want to be recognized for their original ideas and specific skills, rather than for their overall performance. The democratic leader, on the other hand, has the authority to make the final choice. This method may be most effective in situations where interpersonal relationships are of key importance (see Reference 2).

THE LAIZZEZ-ORGANIZING FAIRE'S COMMITTEE

Laizzez-faire is a French expression that means "leave to do." This leadership style gives employees the freedom to execute their jobs in their own way, with little monitoring or control on their actions. If employees lack confidence and are not self-motivated, a key risk with this leadership style is that they will perform poorly as a result of a lack of direction or guidance. This method may be most effective when applied to highly skilled staff teams (see Reference 3).

THEORIES OF LEADERSHIP IN THE BUSINESS ENVIRONMENT

What is it about some leaders that inspires and influences them, whereas others do not? Over the course of decades, scholars have struggled to find an answer to this conundrum. Leadership theories have arisen over time to describe what leadership is, how it functions, and what it should aim to be. Here are some examples of leadership theories. These beliefs range from the concept of a single "Great Man" whose charm inspires others to follow him to the observation that leadership styles must be tailored to the circumstances and environment in which they are used.

THE GREAT MAN THEORY IS THE FIRST OF THESE THEORIES.

According to the Great Man thesis, leadership is viewed as a heroic deed performed by an individual. That is to say, there's something distinctive about a person's unique combination of characteristics, personality traits, and personal attributes that mark her as a great leader and distinguish her from everyone else.

Alternatively, it might be said that leaders aren't born; they're made.

Despite its simplicity, the Great Man theory is all the more enticing. Leaders have always sought out those who can enthuse and motivate others to work toward a common objective. It doesn't matter if the person has other strengths or faults if they have these features.

THE CHALLENGE OF TRAIT-BASED LEADERSHIP THEORIES IN THE BUSINESS ENVIRONMENT

The Great Man theory holds that a specific set of personality traits, either separately or in combination, might cause a person to be regarded as a "great man" in some way. The challenge is that academics have not been able to identify a universally applicable set of qualities that are associated with effective leadership.

Without a doubt, there are certain personality traits that assist leaders in their roles as leaders. Researchers have discovered that reliability, friendliness, initiative, and self-confidence are characteristics that distinguish some (though by no means all) leaders from the others. Researchers have attempted to add a variety of other characteristics to the list throughout the years, including creativity, extroversion, and conscientiousness, to mention a few. However, they have failed to demonstrate a consistent pattern of characteristics that are necessary for leadership effectiveness.

The absence of empirical backing for trait-based hypotheses is not the only issue that has to be addressed. Other criticisms leveled at this approach include: The Great Man theory is based solely on character traits and does not take into account the behavior of the individual. It does not take into account the individual's work environment and his or her particular situation, which has a significant impact on the individual's leadership potential. One of the most common misconceptions about leadership is that various personality attributes are required for different situations. To lead a community-based nonprofit organization, for example, requires a different set of personal characteristics than leading a multinational, profit-driven corporation. The Great Man theory's goal of discovering universal characteristics of leadership remains unattainable, and it is still controversial in the scientific community.

THE SECOND THEORY IS CALLED THE BEHAVIORAL THEORY.

Behavioral forms of leadership theories – of which there are many – are those that are concerned with how leaders behave in their own organizations. As an example, do they yell orders at their employees and expect them to follow through on their instructions? Or do they work in collaboration with their staff to make decisions?

- The Good Man Theory is the polar opposite of behavioral theory, which holds that good leaders can be developed rather than merely born.
- The Lewin Theory of Behavioral Leadership is a theory that describes how people behave in certain situations.

Kurt Lewin's work on leadership behavior has stood the test of time better than any other model of leadership that has been produced over the years. Leaders, according to Lewin, can be classified into three categories: authoritarian, democratic, and laissez-faire. The term "Lewin Theory" refers to this method to leadership that is sometimes used.

LEADERSHIP CHARACTERIZED BY AUTOCRACY

Autocratic executives make decisions as if they were dictators, without engaging their teams or other stakeholders. Consider the image of a high-ranking army official yelling orders for the rank and file soldiers to obey. This is an excellent representation of the autocratic style of leadership in use today.

With this style of leadership, decision-making is speedy, which makes it particularly beneficial for short-duration projects with a very tight deadline in which the firm must make decisions as soon as possible. Communication, on the other hand, is one-way, which can annoy employees and lead to dependency as people come to rely on their boss to make all of the important choices.

DEMOCRATIC PARTY IN CHARGE

As a result, democratic or participative leadership solicits feedback from the team before making decisions, and the team bears equal responsibility for the decision and its results. A beneficial leadership style in organizations that practice continuous process improvement, where it is vital to solicit input from all parties involved in the process in order to determine what is working and which elements are not.

Democratic leadership is related with a positive working environment for employees because people are encouraged to express their ideas and take ownership of the decisions that the company is making under their direction. Decision-making, on the other hand, can be delayed, which permits a weak leader to slip between the cracks of the team's joint efforts.

LEADERSHIP THAT IS "LAISSEZ-FAIRE"

Laissez-faire is a French expression that means "allow individuals to do what they want." As the name implies, these leaders do not intervene and instead enable staff to just carry out their responsibilities in whichever manner they see fit. This type of leadership is effective when the team is strongly motivated and capable of doing good work without the need for constant supervision and intervention.

Giving employees the autonomy they need to accomplish their best work can provide them with the independence they need to do their best work, and it reduces the amount of work the leader has to do as a result. Employees, on the other hand, can become anxious if they are not properly supported, and there is a possibility that no one will be willing to step up and accept responsibility if something goes wrong.

THE SITUATIONAL LEADERSHIP THEORY IS THE THIRD TYPE OF LEADERSHIP THEORY.

While situational leadership is defined as "the realization that the most effective leaders adjust their behaviors based on the environment," it is not a specific style of leadership. For example, a leader who is sent in to manage a crisis situation may be required to steer the ship with an autocratic hand, but a leader in charge of a team of specialists may be required to empower the team to discuss, collaborate, and manage their own decision-making processes.

MODEL DEVELOPED BY HERSEY AND BLANCHARD

The Hersey and Blanchard model of situational leadership is likely the most well-known of all the situational leadership styles and theories. Leaders who adapt and advance in response to the demands of followers, according to the theories of these two authors,: Focus on followers rather than the larger working environment; Respond to the demands of their flock by altering their behavior;

As a tool, the Hersey-Blanchard model goes beyond theory. Leaders can use it to determine the maturity level of their followers and, as a result, the leadership style to apply in a given situation based on this information. According to this definition, "followers" refers to a group of employees who have similar degrees of competency (ability) and commitment (willingness to perform the job).

ACCORDING TO LOGIC, THE FOUR CATEGORIES OF EMPLOYEES ARE AS FOLLOWS:

- Low maturity (low competence/low commitment) these personnel are hesitant and unable to complete work on their own initiative and require very specific instructions on how to perform their jobs properly. Instructional, directive, and autocratic leadership styles are all appropriate in the right situation.
- These individuals have low-to-medium maturity (low competence/high dedication). They are motivated, but may be unable, to accomplish duties on their own initiative. The right leadership style is that of a salesperson: persuasive, encouraging, and motivating others.
- Average maturity (high competence/low commitment) these individuals are competent of performing duties on their own, but they are apprehensive about taking on more responsibility. Involved, team-based, and consultative leadership styles are the most fit for the job description.

- High maturity (high competence/high commitment) indicates that these employees are capable and eager to accomplish things on their own initiative. Leadership styles that are appropriate for delegation include trusting, empowering, and being laissez-faire.

THE FOURTH THEORY OF LEADERSHIP IS TRANSFORMATIONAL LEADERSHIP.

In recent years, there has been a great deal of interest in the final theory of leadership. The transformational model is the one described here. According to this theory, an organization's role is to change, in the sense of bringing new ways of looking at the organization, and more specifically, a vision of what it could and should be, to the fore of the organization. Transformational leadership is concerned with the future of the organization and the adjustments that will be required to improve it.

Transformational leaders, according to James MacGregor Burns, a political scientist who pioneered the theory of transformative leaders in the context of political leadership, can be divided into two categories: transactional and transformational.

When influencing their followers, transactional leaders employ a carrot and stick strategy — they offer incentives while withholding rewards, and win compliance by offering something in exchange for their followers' cooperation. Transformational leaders, on the other hand, are concerned with motivating their followers to assist one another and the organization as a whole, rather than just themselves. Employees respond to their boss with feelings of loyalty, adoration, and trust, and they are eager to put in long hours for the person they admire and respect.

INEFFECTIVE LEADERSHIP IS DEFINED AS FOLLOWS:

Knowledge of good leadership can spell the difference between success and failure in a business. In a wide range of pursuits, such as business, team sports, and politics, ineffective leadership results in disappointment, resignation, and tension among those involved. Ineffective leaders lack the courage to confront challenging issues, and they frequently pass the blame to others. Knowing the characteristics that distinguish ineffective leaders is beneficial since it can serve as a guide for what not to do as a leader in the future.

COMPLACENCY

Ineffective leaders believe that all of the hard work has been completed. They do not believe that any improvements can or should be done in the current situation. Ineffective leaders, in contrast to effective leaders, do not strive to see the world in a different light or to improve their leadership abilities. Because of their complacency, their followers frequently lose respect for them, believing that they are wasting their time by following them. Lack of initiative exhibited by unsuccessful leaders can even be transmitted to their followers, making it more difficult for them to attain success.

THE INABILITY TO COMMUNICATE

What a leader communicates and how she expresses it are both important factors in deciding whether or not she is effective as a leader. Those in charge of ineffective organizations issue directives and deliver instructions that are ambiguous and erroneous. Subordinates and other team members frequently have difficulties comprehending the motivations of their superiors behind some commands since they make little sense and, in some cases, contradict the team's declared goals and objectives. Poor communication extends beyond the words of leaders as well. Communication is an important part of setting a good example. Ineffective leaders say one thing and then do something very different. Because ineffective leaders lose their credibility with their subordinates, they will find it more difficult to persuade team members in the future that they should follow her instructions or actions.

UNCERTAINTY (SEE REFERENCES 1)

For this reason, ineffective leaders frequently struggle to build trust with their followers since they do not set a good example and do not possess the necessary communication skills to accomplish success. Employees or team members who do not trust their bosses or managers are more prone to grow disillusioned and to resign or revolt in some other way. Followers are wary of ineffective leaders because they put them in danger without a justifiable reason, and because they believe they are being used for personal ambitions and avarice rather than the good of the group.

CULPABILITY

Ineffective leaders are unable to accept responsibility for their own faults. They believe that they have the ability to make severe blunders and either shift the responsibility to innocent followers or conceal the seriousness of their errors. Ineffective leaders are unable to acknowledge their own inadequacies because doing so would jeopardize their own competency and ability to manage their teams. Some leaders go so far as to delegate all of their responsibilities to others, so that when a problem arises, they are not held directly responsible for the situation.

LEADING CHANGE REQUIRES SPECIFIC COMPETENCIES

For any people, institution, organization, or business, change is a critical aspect in determining their level of success. Bringing about change in a corporation may be challenging, especially when the needs of employees, higher management, board members, and customers all need to be considered. Those in positions of leadership during periods of transition must acquire the abilities necessary to successfully oversee that transition.

FOR MANAGING CHANGE, USEFUL GOAL-SETTING METHODS

While transitioning an organization, a leader must be able to maintain focus on the organization's broader goals and mission. This man needs to see the big picture before setting goals and deadlines for the change he wants to see in his community. An effective leader must be able to discern how the small pieces fit together to achieve the larger goals and persuade staff to participate in the effort.

ORGANIZATIONAL CAPABILITIES FOR CHANGE MANAGEMENT

Developing organizational skills is essential while managing change in an organization. These skills will allow you to keep track of the changes that need to be made, the timetables for implementing procedural changes, and the people or clients who will be affected by the changes. Develop the ability to assign some tasks to others in order to effectively lead through change. Develop the ability to outsource control of some components of the process to trusted personnel. Provide monitoring when necessary, but give others the opportunity to push, develop, and demonstrate their abilities.

INTERPERSONAL SKILLS REQUIRED FOR CHANGE MANAGEMENT

It is vital to properly implement organizational transformation that all relationships are handled with care. It is also critical to establish positive and open working relationships with other members of management, board members, and clients, among other things. Individuals should be treated with kindness and respect, and their needs should be accommodated whenever possible. When it is vital to be tough and adhere to one's convictions, do so with kindness and consideration for the impact that your actions will have on everyone concerned.

COMMUNICATION AND LISTENING SKILLS

Employees' concerns, frustrations, and ideas should be heard and taken into consideration by a leader as he develops plans and establishes objectives. It is simple to alienate employees by dismissing their concerns and opinions; therefore, it is important to remember that they are an essential part of implementing successful change in an organization. Display effective listening skills by making eye contact, leaning forward in interest, asking clarifying questions, and fully engaging your intellect in order to comprehend what is being spoken. Even if people do not agree with the final decision, they are more likely to continue to fulfill their responsibilities in the implementation of the decision if they believe that their input has been taken into account.

LEADING BY EXAMPLE IN A GROUP SITUATION

It is not necessary to be the project manager in order to lead the team. Anyone can take the initiative and assume a leadership position. You may have an impact on outcomes, regardless of your position in the organization, by recognizing and grabbing leadership opportunities when they present themselves. Influencing without direct authority entails creating a large network of contacts, understanding how to persuade colleagues, bargaining with stakeholders, consulting with others to carry out initiatives, and forming coalitions of like-minded individuals. Waiting for an official promotion or title to manage change, innovate, and reduce stress for others is a waste of time. Instead, set a good, positive example for your teammates by acting in a proactive manner.

CARRY OUT THE TASK

People automatically admire and respect team members who put in the effort. If you want to be seen as a leader in your organization, you must do your job well and accept more responsibility. Building trust and building credibility will assist you in developing your leadership presence, dignified demeanor, and gravitas, among other qualities. A leader takes on the most difficult assignments and forges the connections that are required to solve complex problems. Set a good example by practicing discipline, such as arriving on time for meetings, staying late if a task needs to be completed, and offering to assist a colleague who appears to be struggling to meet an upcoming deadline.

KEEP YOUR PHRASES TO A MINIMUM

Subordinates benefit from the feedback provided by effective leaders. They accomplish this by carefully selecting their words in order to maintain morale and relationships. Taking an active role in resolving little difficulties before they become major ones is an important part of leading by example. In order to assist team members in resolving interpersonal issues, it is necessary to communicate openly while avoiding stoking further conflict. In addition to setting an example, it is important to provide constructive feedback on a coworker's performance when it is necessary, but in a private and diplomatic manner. As a bonus, leading without authorship implies that you will always respect the established hierarchy and will never deliberately undermine the current leadership.

TAKE YOUR TIME TO LISTEN

In addition, knowing how to react in challenging situations is a must for most positions of leadership. Autocratic leaders make all of their decisions on their own. Before making changes that will have an impact on the team, Democratic leaders seek input from the team. Leading by example may entail taking a step back and actively listening to the concerns and arguments of team members. In this way, leaders are able to gather feedback, which allows them to direct activities for the team from a more realistic perspective. Team members' knowledge resides in their heads, and great leaders understand that encouraging them to open up and brainstorm ideas can help increase productivity on the job.

MEMBERS OF THE TEAM SHOULD BE REWARDED.

Some members of the squad love receiving public acclaim for their accomplishments. It is acceptable for team members to express gratitude to other team members for their efforts, insights, and new tactics, even if they do not occupy a managerial position. A team member might acquire the respect of his or her teammates by showing them the same courtesy. This boosts morale and elevates her as a leader in the organization. There are many ways she may inspire the team and earn their respect simply by being polite and generous.

TRANSFORMATIONAL LEADERSHIP HAS ITS CONS, BUT IT ALSO HAS ITS CONS

The world would be a wonderful place if everyone could come together and work cohesively to push a firm towards its ultimate outcome. Essentially, this is the cornerstone of a management style known as transformational leadership, which involves bringing everyone into the decision-making process and ensuring that everyone is personally committed in the success of the organization. That sounds fantastic, doesn't it? However, if you're considering implementing this method in your company, it's critical to understand both the shortcomings and the virtues of transformational leadership.

CONFUSION SURROUNDS LEADERS

Despite the fact that employees have expressed a preference for transformational leadership styles, one study found that many employers were merely pretending to provide them. However, from the perspective of the employees, the leadership style was transactional, which is the polar opposite of transformational. When it comes to leadership styles, transactional leadership styles attempt to exchange rewards for performance rather than considering employees as actual participants in the decision-making process. Instead of continuing to treat employees as subordinates, transformational leaders must ensure that they are truly focusing on team-building and cooperation rather than on individual performance.

IT IS DEPENDENT ON THE EMPLOYEES.

The dynamics of teams might range considerably from one company to the next, therefore one solution will not work for every organization. Employees who wish to be a part of the process and who also work well with one another are the ideal candidates for transformational leadership. If a leader discovers that convening the complete team in one place to discuss major changes results in a lack of involvement or frequent conflict, this method is most certainly not the best fit for the situation at hand.

WHEN PASSION TAKES THE PLACE OF REASON

Some of the most inspirational leaders have been able to win over vast numbers of people with concepts that appear to be "transformational." Followers get enthralled by the leader's zeal, believing that he or she has the potential to make a significant impact in their life. The message of a transformational leader, on the other hand, is not always a sound one. It is critical for a leader to not only involve team members in company operations, but to also listen to their opinions and suggestions.

TRYING TO AVOID BEING A FAVORITE

Could you treat each member of a team equally if you were in charge of a group of individuals working toward a common goal? Trying to prevent preferential treatment is challenging, especially when you're trying to solicit ideas from your team's members. Natural selection will produce more contributors, some of whom may provide better value in their efforts, and you may find yourself paying more attention to these individuals than you would have expected to do so. Leadership must make a concerted effort to incorporate everyone in order for transformational leadership to empower the entire team. This may entail mentoring less experienced team members at times.

Despite the fact that transformational leadership has its drawbacks, it is possible to achieve success with the correct commitment. It is the responsibility of leaders to monitor the results of this approach and ensure that they are achieving the desired results. Over time, you will be able to identify the type of leadership style that is most effective for your particular team, even if that means combining a number of different ways.

WHAT EXACTLY IS THE TRAIT APPROACH?

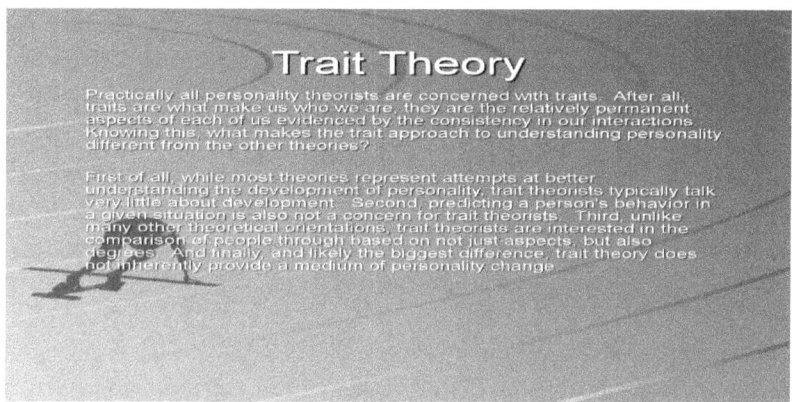

Have you ever wondered what makes a leader different from a follower, or what personality traits they possess? There are several alternative theories of leadership, each of which provides slightly different solutions to these issues. The trait method, for example, is predicated on the notion that people are born with distinct personality qualities that stay consistent across time, as opposed to the trait approach. According to this notion, leaders are born with certain abilities and characteristics that enable them to excel in their occupations and distinguish themselves from the crowd.

UNDERSTANDING THE TRAIT THEORY DEVELOPED BY GORDON ALLPORT

The trait approach, often known as the trait theory of leadership, is credited to Gordon Allport, who was one of the pioneers of personality physiology in the 1950s and 1960s. His research began in the 1930s, when he collected a list of 4,500 personality qualities, which he divided into three categories: central characteristics, cardinal characteristics, and secondary characteristics.

Integrity, kindness, shyness, intelligence, and other fundamental characteristics influence an individual's personality and actions. Cardinal characteristics, on the other hand, characterize a person; Albert Einstein, for example, was renowned for his great intellect, but Martin Luther King, Jr. was renowned for his strong sense of justice and righteousness. The presence of secondary characteristics only occurs in specific contexts, and this may explain why most people react differently whether they are under stress, excited, furious, or any other emotion. Let's repeat that. Transparency doesn't come through systems or procedures; it comes from your leadership.

Allport's trait theory is based on the assumption that each human has a distinct psychological structure and that certain characteristics are associated with effective leadership. To put it another way, outstanding leaders are born rather than created. Several more hypotheses, such as the Myers–Briggs Type Indicator, the Big Five model, and Hans Eysenck's three-factor model, have been developed over the years. Human personality is described by five personality traits, such as conscientiousness and extroversion, according to the Big Five theory, which is popular today.

The Trait Approach to Leadership is a way of looking at how people behave.

In the early twentieth century, psychologists attempted to understand what distinguishes effective leaders from unsuccessful ones, as well as what makes them successful. Certain personality traits such as confidence, adaptability, initiative, honesty, emotional intelligence, and charisma are said to distinguish outstanding leaders and can be used to predict leadership effectiveness, according to the trait theory.

Researchers such as Ralph Stogdill, Michael M. Lombardo, Morgan W. McCall, and others have found many characteristics, talents, and qualities that all good leaders share. These include the following:

- Assertiveness is a character trait.
- Perseverance is required.
- The ability to bounce back from adversity.
- Extremely high levels of energy.
- High levels of judgment and decision-making ability.
- Having self-assurance is important.
- A strong sense of purpose and motivation
- Honesty is the best policy.
- Intelligence is a phrase used to characterize one's capacity for gathering and analyzing data.
- Creativity is essential.
- The ability to understand business concepts.
- Possessing strong interpersonal abilities.
- Emotional stability is important.
- Adaptable to changing events and circumstances.
- The ability to use tact and diplomacy.

- The urge to take the initiative.

The attribute approach to leadership is based on the assumption that leaders are born with certain characteristics. For example, a person who lacks confidence will not be able to develop confidence over time and will therefore be unable to serve as an effective leader. Trait theory is also used by researchers in criminology and other domains to develop psychological profiles of individuals and better understand why they behave the way they do.

THE TRAIT THEORY HAS SOME LIMITATIONS.

Because of its capacity to define distinct personality traits and understand how they influence human behavior, this theory is very useful. This was one of the first attempts to investigate the nature of leadership and the aspects that contribute to its effectiveness. Modern research, on the other hand, challenges these conclusions.

In the first place, the trait theory credits more than 100 different characteristics, including physical characteristics, to effective leaders. These are merely broad generalizations that may or may not apply to all outstanding leaders in the world. Furthermore, it is difficult to describe a "good" leader without being subjective in one's assessment.

When it comes to leadership, the trait theory is all on the leader and doesn't take the situation into consideration. In one setting, the personality traits listed above can assist individuals in emerging as leaders; yet, in another situation, they may not be as effective. In other words, just because you have the skills and experience to lead a small team does not imply that you have the skills and experience required to manage an entire department. Additionally, many of the characteristics listed can be learned and improved via practice and instruction.

SIGNS OF SMALL BUSINESS LEADERSHIP

Being a leader for your small business entails carrying out a variety of practical responsibilities. Keeping your expectations realistic and encouraging your employees to achieve defined goals with demonstrable outcomes is essential. Another component of being a leader is making symbolic efforts. These have the effect of inspiring or enlightening employees. You set the tone by setting an example, and you have faith that the practical application of what you do will emerge when employees follow your lead. Leaders that are skilled in symbolism can bring their teams together and successfully steer their companies.

PUTTING YOURSELF IN A CONFIDENT POSITION

Symbolic leadership necessitates maintaining one's composure even in difficult circumstances. If you walk around the office with your shoulders slouching and a worried expression on your face, you are symbolically representing the anxieties that your coworkers may be experiencing. Instead, you can stand with your shoulders squared, your eyes fixed on others, and a grin on your face. Your certain demeanor can serve as a symbol of confidence for employees who require comfort from your presence.

ACCEPTING AND EMBRACING CHANGE

Change can be demoralizing for your employees. Employees who are faced with new bosses, new methods of doing things and new processes may feel unsure about their capacity to adjust to the new environment. In these kinds of situations, symbolic action can be taken. For example, you may convene a meeting and toss out all of the old logos for a product that has been discontinued. For example, you could walk arm in arm with new managers, or you may directly display a new manufacturing procedure. This demonstrates that you are willing to make adjustments and that it is possible.

AUTHENTICITY

Employees have a tendency to admire leaders that are not just authoritative, but also genuine in their approach. A leader who retains the same temperament in private as she does in public presents herself as a figure of stability to her followers. If a leader is conducting an employee review, she should adopt the same tone of voice, mannerisms, and values that she does when speaking to the entire group of employees. Employees can feel confident in a leader's ability to treat everyone the same way because of this symbolic constancy. Your office décor should include photographs of you with family and friends, as well as photographs taken while on vacation. This represents the fact that you carry your personal life to the job and that you do not have two different lifestyles for work and home.

THE CORNER OFFICE IS A POSITION OF AUTHORITY.

The size and location of offices have long been used to convey a sense of authority and importance. It is possible that your huge corner office will help you reach your objectives if you need to remind staff that is in charge. A less glamorous workplace may be better suited to your preferred leadership style if you value teamwork above individual achievement. In a symbolic way, this will signal to them your view of yourself as one of them.

NOTES WRITTEN BY HAND

When a boss writes a handwritten note to congratulate an employee, he or she is sending a symbolic representation of his or her personal interest in that individual. Whereas email previously displaced the handwritten note, its scarcity has come to symbolize love and caring among those who receive it. Even when expressing condolences verbally, handwritten notes are a meaningful sign of your sentiments.

Celebrations organizing company-wide celebrations for employee successes might serve as a symbol of your company's appreciation for its staff. This can communicate to others that you not only appreciate their efforts, but that you are also keeping track on the development of your projects.

FACTORS THAT INFLUENCE THE EFFECTIVENESS OF AN ORGANIZATION'S BEHAVIOR

Small-business owners cannot control many of the factors that influence their employees' conduct when they are away from their places of employment, but they can manage their employees' behavior when they are on the job. You can establish criteria for individual employee behavior as well as for how employees behave in groups. You'll also need methods for motivating employees to comply with company policies so that they'll be less inclined to deviate from them.

WHAT IT DOES AND HOW IT WORKS

Consider the factors that influence the behaviors and decisions of employees. Individual and group conduct is taught to children and adolescents by their parents, teachers, other adults, and their peers. Rules can be expressed verbally, written, or implicit. Conditions dictate different standards of behavior than in other circumstances. The essential demands of workers — such as those for food, water, safety, and enjoyment — must be balanced with what they find intriguing as well as the social rules that they have learned over time. The needed behaviors for your corporate culture are taught to employees by you, in particular, because you are the leader whom they must satisfy in order to progress further in their roles.

THE ENVIRONMENT IS BEING CREATED

Employees must become familiar with the norms of your company's culture. Provide a clear environment with clear expectations to assist them in their endeavors. Some expectations are common to all employees, while others are exclusive to a particular role or group of employees. When a position announcement is made, the socialization process begins. It continues through the hiring process, new employee orientation, and performance management by the employee's immediate supervisor or manager.

THE MANAGEMENT'S FUNCTION

Promote individuals who are capable of encouraging others to managerial positions if your company has grown to the point where you can no longer monitor everyone on your own team anymore. These individuals will require emotional intelligence, which includes the capacity to develop ties with employees and motivate them to work at their highest levels of performance. Organizational guidelines for clothing, acting, speaking, communicating electronically, and representing the company in public can be developed with the assistance of managers and employees. Make guidelines for meetings, team projects, and other activities that will take place in a group. When groups establish their own norms, they are more likely to feel a sense of ownership over them throughout group interactions.

CHANGE MANAGEMENT IS A WORD THAT REFERS TO THE PROCESS OF BRINGING ABOUT CHANGES IN A BUSINESS ENVIRONMENT.

In order for senior leaders to be effective, they must persuade employers that patterns of conduct that are counterproductive should be eradicated. This begins with deciding on a new pattern of behavior and continues with replacing the old pattern of behavior with the new pattern of behavior after that decision has been made. Encourage others to follow your lead and embrace the new pattern of conduct. Others will soon follow your lead, and you will be admired.

MOTIVATION

Some factors influencing employees — such as economic pressures, family pressures, current events, employee health and mental well-being, and competition from other companies — are beyond your control; however, you can influence the organizational culture and the way those factors impact work performance by changing it. Ensure that your staffs find the balance between what inspires them and what is expected of them. Extrinsic rewards for employees who follow regulations — such as recognition, promotions, and bonuses — should be provided, while employees who do not follow rules should be subjected to disciplinary action. It is not acceptable to disregard forbidden activities on the grounds that employees are doing what is best for the company. If you want your staff to take the rules seriously, you need to consistently enforce behavioral standards.

IMPROVEMENTS IN CORPORATE CULTURE ARE BEING IMPLEMENTED.

Your employees devote a considerable percentage of their time and energy to ensuring the success of your company. It is critical that they feel wanted and that their efforts are recognized and rewarded. Employees that are content and happy at their jobs are more productive and are more likely to stay with the company for a longer period of time. The company culture is a significant component in determining an employee's overall morale, and strengthening it can have a favorable impact on your company's bottom line.

Making work enjoyable can have a major impact on your company's culture. Tasteful, suitable humor can make a significant difference. According to a recent report, many people are afraid to be amusing or to joke around at their place of employment. According to studies, when people are encouraged to utilize humor, they tend to relax a little more and be more themselves. Whatever you do to help your employees feel more happy about their time spent at the workplace will most likely result in them being more motivated to spend time at the office when you require them during peak hours of company activity, as well. You may need to regulate your comedy as closely as you would any other element of your life in order to ensure that it does not cross the line into something inappropriate or absorb too much of your time.

RECOGNIZE AND CELEBRATE YOUR ACCOMPLISHMENTS AND PASSIONS

Inviting employees to know that you are interested in their lives outside of work will help them feel valued and have a more positive attitude on your organization. Consider Kathleen, an account manager at ABC Corporation who has a son who has epilepsy and who volunteers for the Epilepsy Foundation. Kathleen is a good example. If she is never recognized for her accomplishments or her passions, she may come to believe that she is nothing more than a number to ABC Corporation, rather than a real person with a unique personality. Her coworkers may never be able to connect with her on topics that are not related to work. This can have a negative impact on the company's culture.

Instead, take time to recognize and celebrate the particular accomplishments and passions of each of your employees. It is beneficial to your company culture when you treat your employees as if they are important to you beyond their contributions to your organization.

POSITIVE THINKING AND COLLABORATIVE ACTION ARE ESSENTIAL.

The mind is an extremely strong tool. Poor ideas result in negative attitudes, which might spread to other members of the organization... Companies with cultures that encourage innovative and positive thinking also assist their staff in developing positive thinking and meditative skills. In addition, foster a collaborative environment by breaking away from the usual routine and encouraging individuals to work together on projects.

COMMUNICATE

Above all, interact with your staff in an open and honest manner, and listen to their problems. In the midst of the day-to-day hustle and bustle of business operations, it is easy to become distracted or overwhelmed by other difficulties, making it difficult to pay attention to your company's culture. However, even if you just have a few minutes every day to listen to your staff and show them that you care, spending the effort to do so can reap significant rewards in the long run. Take a few minutes to speak with your staff, listen to their issues, and then act if necessary to address them.

WHAT TO DO WHEN YOU HAVE A SUBORDINATE

Master-servant relationships, also known as the supervisor-employee relationships, are always being debated, considered, and renewed in today's workplace. When a supervisor is just elevated to supervisory status and is in charge of employees who were once their peers, it might be challenging for them to deal with a subordinate effectively. Supervisors also have difficulties dealing with subordinates who refuse to follow job orders and who are insubordinate in their behavior. One of the difficulties supervisors face is maintaining a leadership role rather than attempting to gain popularity. They may also be hesitant to provide employees with constructive feedback for fear that the employees will react negatively to feedback intended to help them improve their performance.

COMMUNICATION

There are no excuses for not openly and honestly communicating with your employees if you want to be a good manager. When there is no regular, two-way communication between you and your staff, it is difficult to verify that your employees understand your performance expectations as they change. An employee's high-performance rating is unachievable if they do not understand what you and your company demand of them. To build a positive working environment, effective communication with your coworkers must begin with effective communication with yourself. Effective communication is especially crucial when providing constructive criticism to employees regarding their performance flaws and when conducting performance appraisal meetings with employees. Keep bad performance from going unnoticed, and avoid skipping the annual face-to-face meetings with your staff during performance review season to avoid appearing incompetent.

Acknowledgment Management consultant Frederick Herzberg thought that one of the most effective ways to encourage employees was through recognition, which is one of the elements of his two-factor, motivation-hygiene theory, which is one of the elements of his motivation-hygiene theory. One method of motivating subordinates is to provide them with positive reinforcement, such as by assigning them to lucrative jobs when their performance justifies more challenging work and responsibilities. When you delegate more responsibility to your staff, they are more likely to desire to demonstrate that they are deserving of your praise. In other words, they don't want to let you down once you've determined that their skill sets are sufficient to warrant promotion to a higher-level position within the organization.

POPULARITY AMONG SUPERVISORS

When you work as a supervisor, your aim is not to gain more popularity. Although some of your decisions will be controversial, as long as you remain firm on work-related decisions and are able to defend the business reasons that back your decisions, your staff will respect you and follow your lead. A supervisor who is more concerned with being popular with a small group of employees and catering to their whims rather than acting in the best interests of the overall work group is an undesirable option.

AFFIRMATIVE ACTION IN COACHING

Too many organizations have disciplinary procedures that imply a parent-child relationship exists between managers and their employees, which is not the case. In a workplace where adults collaborate, there is no need for an employee to be "punished" or to believe that he or she is "in trouble" for concerns that require adult behavior. Employee coaching, positive reinforcement, and performance counseling should be replaced with terminology that are not centered on discipline but rather on employee development. Keep the use of language and concepts that minimize the importance of employees to the organization to a minimum. Integrate ideas and terminology into your company that express respect for your employees' abilities, skills, and credentials.

LEADERSHIP THAT IS EFFECTIVE

Effective leaders stand to earn as much from their employees as their people stand to benefit from their supervisors in terms of performance. Don't pass up opportunities to learn from those who work under your supervision or report to you. According to management guru John Maxwell, "Leaders must be close enough to relate to others while being far enough ahead to motivate them." This indicates that your work as a supervisor should involve a fluid flow of ideas from your perspective as well as from the perspectives of your subordinates. After all, you and your staff are all striving for the same end result: increased overall productivity and profitability. Putting an excessive amount of gap between yourself and your subordinates will not bring you any closer to the general objectives of the organization.

ETIQUETTE IN THE SUPERVISORY ROLE

When it comes to the workplace, there is always communication and conduct that takes place behind the scenes of actual job duties in action — yet office decorum or the lack thereof, is never something that goes unnoticed, either. When bad manners are on display, they can be seen and felt even if no one is talking about it with you. As a supervisor, your employees are unlikely to bring these concerns to your attention; therefore, be proactive in considering how your behavior is perceived by your staff in order to ensure that everyone feels comfortable.

PAY ATTENTION AND WAIT

Controlling employees' speech is especially important when they are irritated. Before responding to what you've just heard, weigh your options. When answering, be cognizant of the language you use and adhere to the supervisory standards your firm has established. Keep your emotions in check, as they could be seen as an overreaction by others. This will aid in the prevention of legal and ethical concerns in the future. There's always a danger that what you say will be misinterpreted, so remember that whatever you say in the workplace can and will be used against you, no matter how innocent you appear to be. To answer to an employee who has voiced strong feelings toward you, the ideal response would be to say something like, "I'm sorry you feel that way; let's see if we can come up with a solution." Maintain your professional demeanor no matter what your staffs say to you — even if it means engaging in small talk.

KEEP THE LINES DRAWN BETWEEN THINGS.

Particularly during periods of high stress at the workplace, it is easy to become entangled in office gossip or snide remarks. Most of the time, someone manages to divulge information about their personal lives outside of work. As the boss, you must, on the other hand, mentally note when it is appropriate to shift the subject of a conversation to work-related issues or to simply walk away from a chat. Employees should not interact with one another outside of the workplace, whether at bars or on social networking sites. Employees who are outgoing or pushy may easily get you into talking about yourself as well, so be aware that crossing limits might lead to issues for you later on, when workplace gossip spreads tales about your company. The same can be said about physical proximity between two points. It is never, ever acceptable to physically contact an employee, even if it is to pat them on the back or tap their arm; the wrong person on the wrong day might convert it into a sexual harassment complaint or simply feel uncomfortable.

BE CONSIDERATE AND COURTEOUS.

Employees' propensity to perform effectively for you is likely to be influenced by their impression of you. On days when work is onerous and stress levels are high, employees feel more at peace if they are treated in a pleasant manner. Make eye contact and smile when you see them in the corridor or go past their desk — but don't go overboard. Refrain from admiring or rewarding them for their appearance if you don't want to risk disciplinary action if they do an outstanding job on a task or project. You can demonstrate your appreciation for their efforts by treating them to lunch in order to commemorate their achievements and to express your admiration for their dedication.

THE PRIVACY SHOULD BE RESPECTED.

When working with your subordinates one-on-one, proper business etiquette for bosses dictates that you show respect for them. Taking this into consideration, you must provide your staff with a break if they need to get something to eat or use the restroom, make a phone call, or visit the doctor. If people believe that they are being micromanaged for their personal behavior or the work that they accomplish, they are more prone to develop feelings of resentment. Because you probably have more privacy in your workspace than they do, they may not have the luxury of hiding behind closed doors in an office the way you do. Allow them to have their own place, and they will thank you for it. Likewise, if they are taking advantage of you and failing to meet your expectations at work, the conversation you have with them to correct the situation should take place in private so that they do not embarrass themselves in front of their coworkers.

HOW DO CHARISMATIC LEADERSHIP AND SUBORDINATE PERFORMANCE INTERACT?

According to "Psychology Today," charismatic leaders are born with the ability to inspire and motivate others. These supervisors are frequently successful in enhancing the quality of their employees' work. According to the American Society for the Advancement of Project Management, the concern with this leadership style is that if the manager is primarily motivated by self-image rather than corporate goals, her techniques may become unduly autocratic and counterproductive to the requirements of her employees.

INSPIRATION ON A CYCLICAL BASIS

Leaders who are naturally charismatic make a powerful first impression on their subordinates and colleagues. According to the Business Perspectives website, charisma is associated with something new and exciting, which is particularly important for struggling organizations. Staff employees respond positively to this style of manager's charm, persuasion, and extroverted demeanor by being more productive and energized. When the leader is recognized by the business community in which he or she works, this might fuel the leader's ambitions for further growth. In his talks to subordinates, he will use his magnetic personality to motivate them to strive toward his vision. As a result, the relationship between leaders and employees is cyclical in nature, with each entity attempting to impress the other.

EMOTIONAL ATTACHMENT

The bond that develops between charismatic bosses and their employees happens swiftly. Employees are naturally drawn to a boss who they believe is personally invested in them and the company's future. University of Houston Victoria researchers have discovered that leaders who exude charm have deep emotional bonds with their followers. Charismatic leaders are able to readily show their empathy and concern for the people with whom they interact. These managers persuade employees in group situations as well as one-on-one meetings that they are important to her personally, regardless of whether or not this is actually the case. Workers perform better under the direction of leaders with whom they have developed a personal connection. Employee backlash can result in bad performance if the leader is found to be fake, as these employees' exhibit animosity and disappointment towards the leader.

HAVING A SPIRITUAL EXPERIENCE

Despite the fact that the connection between managers and employees is primarily one of business, a charismatic leader has the ability to have nearly supernatural power over his or her followers. According to "Psychology Today," the ability of a charismatic leader to inspire people is a fundamental characteristic of this management style. The majority of those who work for this type of manager describe their connection with them as one of "serving" visionary leaders. Employees' performance improves when they have faith in their boss, but they can lose faith in the entire organization if a charismatic leader fails to live up to his or her promises to them.

DESIGNING WITH A VARIETY OF STYLES

When it comes to charismatic leadership, it is often more similar to traditional authoritarian management than to participatory management approaches that allow employees to share in decision-making responsibilities and learn to be leaders themselves. Combined with empowering methods that guide employee growth and professionalism, the naturally charismatic leader will likely be able to achieve greater success than she would under a single management approach. "I'm a naturally charismatic leader," says the leader. This blending of styles does necessitate the leader's putting aside her tendency toward egotistic recognition in favor of a role that serves her indirectly, as the business is viewed as more of a group effort than an individual endeavor.

TRANSPARENCY IN THE LEADERSHIP

Almost all employees say that openness in their organization's leadership is towards the top of their list of most important work concerns when asked what they care about the most at work. Despite this, one-third of those who responded to a recent study stated that "their employer is not always honest and truthful with them." These findings are disappointing because transparency in leadership has the potential to produce great achievements that benefit everyone in the firm.

WHAT DOES IT MEAN TO BE TRANSPARENT IN YOUR LEADERSHIP?

Maintaining employee communication, sharing both the good and the bad (yet not oversharing), and soliciting candid input from team members are all examples of transparency in leadership. The absence of unpleasant surprises, uncertainty-related issues, and ambiguous actions that could damage a leader's reputation are all desirable outcomes for any leader. Transparent leaders make it a point to put their words into action, to set clear expectations, and to communicate effectively with each and every person of their organizations.

The ability to lead with transparency involves a desire to be honest and upfront with personnel, even if doing so puts the leader's position in a vulnerable position. In a situation where employees can see and evaluate everything a leader does, it is critical that he or she leads the organization with integrity and in a manner that is consistent with the organization's values. Employees will reciprocate by demonstrating their loyalty and trust.

In leading with openness, an individual sets a high bar for the rest of the organization to follow. As it develops a workplace culture of open communication and accountable behavior for both employees and leaders, the relevance of transparency in leadership becomes increasingly obvious.

TRANSPARENT LEADERSHIP HAS A LOT OF ADVANTAGES

It is possible for a company to reap multiple benefits when it recognizes the value of openness in leadership and continuously executes this practice.

INCREASED EMPLOYEE PARTICIPATION

Inviting employees to provide feedback when a leader chooses to be open and honest with them can help them feel valued. By demonstrating to employees how much the organization values their contributions and ideas, a leader establishes a foundation of trust and loyalty that fosters increased employee advocacy, which in turn contributes to the development of the employer's reputation. Showing attention and gratitude, on the other hand, might help to humanize leaders, making them more relatable in the eyes of their staff. Transparent leaders will gain greater understanding and support from their employees by presenting themselves as actual human beings (rather than as mysterious bosses hidden behind intimidating office doors). Employees will be more willing to accept negative news or open themselves up to constructive feedback if they feel they have a personal connection with their leaders.

EXPECTATIONS THAT ARE WELL-MANAGED

Withholding information frequently results in misconceptions and expectations that are not met. Employee and employer expectations are adequately set and fulfilled when leaders lead with transparency. Clear, open, and frequent communication reduces the likelihood that employees would form incorrect assumptions about their jobs or their employers' organizations.

PERFORMANCE OF THE WORKFORCE HAS IMPROVED.

As increased openness encourages greater employee advocacy, these highly engaged individuals are more likely to achieve higher levels of performance and productivity in their respective positions of responsibility.

HOW TO BE A MORE TRANSPARENT LEADER (WITH EXAMPLES)

Making the transition to becoming a more transparent leader may necessitate some careful adjustments to one's management style (and it may take some time for the advantages to spread throughout the organization), but the results will be well worth the effort.

Put in place a consistent policy for leaders to follow when it comes to being transparent about business developments or choices.

Hold regular meetings with the entire firm, each department, and individual employees to ensure that everyone is up to date on new developments, that clear expectations have been established, and that every employee has the opportunity to be kept informed.

Encourage employees to provide candid feedback on company policies, as well as on any recent changes or announcements that have taken place. In order to acquire this information, you might want to consider conducting an employee satisfaction survey.

Encourage team members in senior management to follow suit by establishing an open door policy.

You should spend some time establishing a working relationship with your personnel by meeting with them one-on-one. Build personal ties with your staff and demonstrate your openness and honesty by taking advantage of this chance.

To begin with, understanding the need of transparency in leadership is the first step in achieving it in the first instance. The moment that leaders make a personal commitment to greater transparency and begin working toward it immediately, they and their organizations are already well on their way to reaping the benefits of greater transparency and openness in their operations.

DEVELOPING A TRANSPARENCY-ORIENTED CULTURE

When direct reports say things like "I'd go to hell and back for my boss," you know they are working for a terrific leader. What kinds of behaviors does a leader need to exhibit in order to inspire that degree of trust and loyalty? Imagine the potential that this formula would have if we were able to bottle it and use it to transform entire organizations.

The actions and behaviors of a leader in establishing a culture of openness help to create a working climate that fosters trust, employee participation, and organizational commitment.

Many books discuss systems, forms of communication, and procedures to use in order to achieve greater transparency in business transactions.

Those are vital tools, but they are insufficient if the leader does not regularly act in ways that enlist willing people to help the organization achieve its strategic objectives. Let's repeat that. Transparency doesn't come through systems or procedures; it comes from your leadership.

1. SHOW OTHERS THAT YOU CARE.

Leaders must answer the unspoken question that permeates their employees' minds on a daily basis: "Do you care about me?" When employees feel seen, acknowledged, confirmed, and encouraged, that question transforms into a conviction: "I will follow you because I am confident that you will assist me in achieving my goals." To accomplish this, leaders must intentionally foster their relationships with direct reports and ensure that employees have access to the resources they need to advance their careers.

Human beings thrive when they are able to establish and maintain intimate ties.

Building relationships fosters feelings of security, understanding, gratitude, and dependability.

What people anticipate from their leaders is frequently encapsulated within these fundamental interpersonal leader-follower relationships. Some business leaders are under the impression that these qualities are not important in a workplace setting. Something further from the truth can't possibly exist.

When leaders build and maintain this foundation, strategic goals have a better chance of being realized.

2. ALLOW YOURSELF TO BE VULNERABLE.

Some leaders might flinch at the use of such word, fearing that it will in some way degrade their standing in the eyes of their workers. The majority of employees, on the other hand, highly appreciate a leader who allows them to come to know their leader's true nature.

Credibility is built via vulnerability, which reveals sincerity of being. To assess the ability of employees to effectively comprehend and disseminate the knowledge that is disclosed, leaders must have requisite maturity, judgment, and self-awareness, to name a few requirements. 1.

A vulnerable leader is one who seeks feedback on his or her personal performance, which is a crucial indicator of their vulnerability. Identifying how people perceive them can help leaders better connect their aspirations with reality and make course corrections as needed in order to continue to establish the culture of transparency that they so desperately desire. Being vulnerable in this way also serves as an example for employees, who will learn that feedback is a great instrument for improving performance and developing high-performing teams.

3. BE BRUTALLY HONEST WITH YOURSELF.

In our interviews with employees across campus, we've found that at least half believe their leaders might be more forthright.

Employees now place a high value on workplace environments that eliminate the cloud of unknowns and flaws that often sneak into their heads when it comes to how decisions are made and the consequences of those decisions on them. When leaders refuse to provide information, for whatever reason, they weaken public confidence. Clearly stating that they do not have all of the pieces in place or that they are awaiting additional evidence is a good practice for leaders. This demonstrates respect for employees as well as an understanding of their concerns and desire for information, which is commendable. When people are honest with themselves, it goes a long way toward eliminating the pervasive impression that there are hidden agendas.

One of the best examples of fearless leadership is someone who is willing to openly discuss both the positive and negative aspects of their experiences.

This gives the message to your staff that they are capable of dealing with the information and that they can rely on you to connect the dots for them when the situation calls for it.

4. HAVE DIFFICULT DIALOGUES WITH YOUR CHILDREN.

In order to lead a poor team or organization, you must avoid confronting concerns of performance head-on. As a result of this avoidance, people's confidence and security are eroded. Additionally, it fosters an environment in which people are hesitant to provide their entire commitment. Why? The reason is that employees want a workplace atmosphere in which uncivil interactions, pointless gossiping, finger-pointing, and other behaviors that undermine the teams' ability to achieve their goals and objectives are not tolerated. Being a transparent leader involves ensuring that your colleagues are well aware of your commitment to having those difficult conversations when they are required. There should be no doubt that inconsiderate and disrespectful behavior will not be accepted in this workplace.

5. PAY CLOSE ATTENTION TO THE GENERAL ATMOSPHERE IN THE OFFICE.

It is almost impossible to conduct anything in the job without being influenced by our emotions. They have an impact on our beliefs, behaviors, and attitudes. It conveys the message to employees that leaders are paying attention to these issues and that they care about their experiences in the workplace when leaders are honest in informing them of their attention to these factors. It also heightens a leader's awareness of how her/his own moods might "infect" the team, both favorably and adversely, and how to avoid this.

6. KEEP YOUR WORD ON YOUR PLEDGES.

Leaders who follow through on their promises in the small things generate trust in the larger picture. The tone is set for the entire corporation by this statement. The simple things, such as arriving on time for meetings, responding to emails promptly, and following through on requests made of employees, are examples of the big things. Being a transparent leader in this area implies that you are conveying your promises clearly and concisely to ensure that there are no misconceptions or miscommunications. Using imprecise wording, such as "I will try to make the meeting," or "You will hear from me as soon as possible," is discouraged. Furthermore, you demonstrate to your staff how adopting precise language enhances levels of accountability by setting an example.

7. MAINTAIN YOUR COMPOSURE.

Leaders who exercise self-control, poise, and patience help to reduce workplace anxiety and unpredictability. One's ability to maintain composure is demonstrated through one's attitude, body language, and general presence. Even in the most stressful situations, leaders may identify that a problem is occurring while maintaining their composure and dignity. The ability to remain strong and confident while also smiling frequently and honestly demonstrating a feeling of compassion helps to defuse workplace disruption and instill confidence in employees that a confident, loving, and brave leader is in command during challenging circumstances.

8. DELIVER TERRIBLE NEWS IN A PROFESSIONAL MANNER.

Yes, there are moments when men's (and women's) souls are tested in their roles as leaders. Leaders who downplay difficult situations, place responsibility on others, or outright lie about them, on the other hand, are not establishing cultures of transparency. The ability to deliver bad news effectively exhibits courage, demonstrating that you are a leader who, despite the fact that it is personally difficult, will do what is best for the organization and the team. Because bad news is usually clear to everyone, it is vital to communicate it to employees as soon as possible. Employees should be given as much information as possible without revealing confidential information, and the blame game should be avoided. When employees express concern or appear disturbed, take the time to listen to them so that they feel that you are "in it with them," rather than tossing a sloppy mess on them and walking away from the situation. Keep everyone informed of the steps that need to be taken to address a problem and communicate frequently about where you are in the process of reducing it.

The perception of working in a company where there are no secrets leads to increased connection and investment in the outcomes, as employees believe they are in a relationship-based workplace. The result is that there are no mysteries concerning cash flow, hours worked, what employees wear to work, how promotions are handled, goals and roadmaps, performance expectations, or the value that each team member brings to the table. Being transparent is not something that can be done once and then forgotten about. You must maintain a level of consistency and dependability. While transparency is not always simple and can expose leaders to the possibility of being wrong and being condemned, the benefits of transparency exceed the dangers by a wide margin. Over time, leaders come to understand the importance of transparency and the good influence it has on all they do in their organizations.

IS THERE A STRATEGY IN PLACE FOR EVERY SENIOR LEADER ON YOUR TEAM IN THE EVENT OF AN EMERGENCY?

If you are the company's chief executive officer, you are included in this category.

It amazes me that the response to this question is no even in organizations with more than 100 employees, which is surprising to me. I understand that this can appear to be a theoretically difficult task at a very small firm (fewer than 20 employees), but it should still be considered an aspirational aim. The ability to recognize this someone once you reach 100 should be a necessity for every leader once you reach this milestone.

This should not be construed as a negative development. If you are having this talk with your leadership team (or if you are a member of a leadership team having this conversation) and you are threatening (or feel threatened), you are not getting the point through properly. Recognize that things happen and that people quit organizations at the most inconvenient times. They are killed. They go through a significant personal transformation. They become disinterested. They are stepping down from their position. They are halted at the Canadian/US border by Customs and Border Protection agents and are unable to re-enter the country. The extraterrestrials arrive.

Leaders go through phases where they are more of a doer than a thinker, which is less spectacular. The organization is experiencing a crisis in a particular area, and a leader must devote 100 percent of her time to resolving the problem rather than spending her entire time on management. Another scenario is that the company's attention is drawn to a new product introduction, and a leader who is responsible for multiple facets of the organization devotes all her concentration to one of the three areas she oversees. Alternatively, someone may feel the need for a vacation and decide to go off the grid for two weeks.

As a CEO, you spend a significant amount of your time working "on" the firm rather than "in" the company. At the top of this list should be ensuring that you have the correct leadership team in place and that they are operating in an extremely effective manner. Part of this involves ensuring that everyone on the team has identified a backup person and is not hesitant to call on them at any time.

WHAT IS THE HISTORICAL CONTEXT OF LEADERSHIP THEORY: AUTHENTIC LEADERSHIP

Leadership theories and literature abound, as does the body of knowledge on leadership. On the one hand, we may discover theories that used an intellectual approach in order to produce Authenticity, and on the other hand, we can find theories that do not take an intellectual approach in order to build Authenticity. The approach is to have a clearer awareness of one's own role and of others' expectations about that role in order to consciously work on the character of one's own role in order to satisfy the expectations of others regarding one's own role in the best possible way. Theory dealing with the method to finding one's personal orientation as a leader, developing one's understanding of one's own personality, and what one stands for, and developing one's grasp of authentic leadership are also available.

QUOTES ON BEING A LEADER

The fundamental heart of being a leader is having a vision for what you want to accomplish. You can't sound a trumpet that isn't sure what it is." "Leadership and learning are inextricably linked," says the author. "An excellent leadership objective is to assist those who are performing poorly in improving their performance and to assist those who are performing well in improving their performance even further.

Leadership quotes are the traces and lessons learned by great leaders throughout history. Innovative ideas and unrelenting dedication have made a good difference in the world. If you want to inspire and build a sense of purpose in your followers, use quotes.

Every human being is driven by a desire to lead, to inspire, and to make a positive contribution to the larger good. Your daily activities as a homemaker, student, or manager may need you to delegate and manage tasks inside an organization, among other things. In every one of us is a leader who is constantly pushing limits and setting examples. Leadership, on the other hand, is not a walk in the park; leaders must possess the characteristics that will help them thrive in their particular industries.

> **HERE IS A COLLECTION OF GOOD LEADERSHIP QUOTES FROM SOME OF THE WORLD'S MOST EXCEPTIONAL LEADERS TO HELP YOU BE INSPIRED AND MAINTAIN YOUR INNER LEADER.**

- Take your own route rather than following the way of the majority.

- Allow the crowds to follow you around. - Margaret Thatcher, as stated in a public speech.

- A leader's ability to be inventive and foresighted should be superior to that of his or her subordinates. - Jack Ma is a successful Chinese businessman.

- Great leaders are not motivated by the desire to lead, but rather by the desire to serve their communities and the world. - Myles Munroe & Associates, Inc.

- Despite numerous setbacks, I never lost up hope of being considered for the role. Darwin E. Smith is a novelist and poet from the United States.

- As opposed to increasing the number of followers, I begin by proposing that the job of leadership is to generate even more leaders than are already available. A political activist and author based in the United States, Ralph Nader is known for his work on climate change.

- Developing yourself as a high-quality individual in your own right is the first step toward becoming a leader who attracts similarly high-quality employees. Motivational speaker and author Jim Rohn resides in California with his wife and two children.

- When his supporters aren't even aware of his presence, an effective leader is at his most effective and efficient. Upon completion of his job and achievement of his goal, they will all proclaim, "We did it ourselves." In the words of Lao-Tzu, the Chinese philosopher

- Achieving success is characterized as the ability to bounce back from failure to failure without losing motivation. In his book The Battle of Britain, Winston Churchill says:

- Before you can be a leader, you must first focus on developing your own abilities in order to be successful. When you rise to the position of leader, your capacity to develop people will decide your level of success. - A proverb attributed to Jack Welch

- A happy person does not feel that way because everything in his or her life is wonderful; rather, he or she feels that way because his or her attitude toward everything in his or her life is perfect.- Sundar Pichai,

- Google CEO Integrity, intelligence, and inclusivity are the three most important characteristics of a good leader. We can begin whenever we choose. We can begin anywhere. – Sadhguru

- It doesn't matter when we begin. It doesn't matter where we begin. All that counts is that we take the first step. - Simon Sinek,

- "Start with Why" As we look ahead to the twenty-first century, those who empower others will be the ones who will be seen as leaders. - Bill Gates, founder of Microsoft

- Leadership is not a popularity contest; it is about putting one's ego aside and focusing on the task at hand. Without a position of authority, the goal of the game is to seize the initiative. - Robin S. Sharma & Partners

- Men who insist on doing everything themselves and grabbing all the credit for their efforts will never be great leaders. Andrew Carnegie is credited with the invention of the telephone.

- If you want to enhance the organization, you must first develop yourself, and the organization will rise with you as a result of your efforts. - Indra Nooyi, a.k.a. It is vital to have innovative leadership in order for any endeavor to be successful.

- In the public sector, non-governmental organizations, and the private sector, innovative leadership is essential. The Honorable A. P. J. Abdul Kalam Not a position, but a choice, is what distinguishes leadership. - Stephen Covey,

- "The 7 Habits of Highly Effective People" Leadership is an opportunity to give back to the community. It is not a blaring hornet's cry to be self-important. J. Donald Walters is a writer and poet.

- A true leader uses every subject, no matter how important or sensitive, to guarantee that we emerge from the debate stronger and more united than we were at the start of the debate. - Nelson Mandela,

- In his own words Great leaders can recognize greatness in others even when they are unable to recognize it themselves, and they can guide people to their utmost potential, which they may not even be aware of. - Roy T. Bennett & Associates
- In order to be effective, both leadership and learning must be utilized together. - President John F. Kennedy

- Leadership is the process of resolving difficulties. It is the day that troops cease to bring their issues to your attention that you have ceased to be their leader. They have either lost faith in your ability to assist them or concluded that you do not care. Either scenario represents a leadership failure. - Colin Powell

- Effective leadership is not characterized by delivering speeches or being loved; rather, it is measured by results rather than characteristics. "- Peter F. Drucker, Jr.

- Integrity is without a doubt the most important attribute for a leader to possess. No true success is possible without it, whether on a section gang, on the football field, in the army, or in the boardroom. - President Dwight D. Eisenhower

- When it comes to leadership qualities, integrity is the most valuable and appreciated. Always follow through on your promises. Brian Tracy is a motivational speaker and author.

- A leader's capacity to guide others without using coercion towards a direction or decision that leaves them feeling empowered and accomplished is defined as follows: Lisa Cash Hanson is a writer and poet.

- To be a successful leader, you must leave a legacy that motivates others to dream bigger and achieve their aspirations. Dolly Parton is a country music singer and songwriter from the United States.

- Leaders are cultivated rather than born into positions of authority. They are the result of sustained work, which is the price that all of us must bear in order to attain any good goal in life. - Vince Lombardi,

- Legendary football coach the greatest leader is not always the one who accomplishes the most remarkable feats of achievement. He is the one that inspires individuals to achieve the most extraordinary things in their lives. - President Ronald Reagan

- When it comes to actual leadership, it is not about seeking consensus, but rather about shaping consensus. The Reverend Dr. Martin Luther King, Jr.

- Do not go down the route that may lead you astray. Going off the beaten path and leaving a trail would be preferable. - Ralph Waldo Emerson's

- "An Essay on the Nature of Things" You must make a long-term commitment to excellence as well as a commitment to leadership since that is the only way to achieve excellence. - Azim Premji, a.k.a. Empathy is essential in leadership.

- In order to inspire and empower people's lives, it is necessary to be able to relate to and connect with them on a personal level. - Oprah Winfrey's remark

- Management is concerned with persuading people to do things they do not want to do, whereas leadership is concerned with motivating people to achieve things they never imagined they were capable of doing in the first place. - Apple CEO Steve Jobs

- If you want to be a leader in your field, you must be willing to be misunderstood. - Amazon CEO Jeff Bezos

- Being a good listener is vitally essential to being a successful leader; you must pay attention to those who are on the front lines of the organization. - Richard Branson (via wikipedia)

- Saying no, rather than saying yes, is the art of leadership. It is fairly simple to respond affirmatively. - Prime Minister Tony Blair

- There are three characteristics of great leaders: inside light, inner vision, and inner strength. Amit Ray is a writer who lives in New York City.

- Great leaders are not afraid of obstacles because problems do not break great leaders; rather, they polish them to become even better. - Give Gugu Mona a gift

- The greatest gift of leadership is having a boss who genuinely cares about your success. - Jon Taffer's remark Effective leadership is characterized by a compelling vision, a complete plan, relentless implementation, and a team of brilliant individuals working collaboratively. - Alan Mulally's remark

- Outstanding leaders go out of their way to help their employees feel more confident in their own abilities. Amazing things can happen when people have faith in their own abilities. Sam Walton is a well-known entrepreneur and philanthropist who founded the Walton Family Foundation.

- I believe that one of the most important aspects of leadership is the recognition that everyone has abilities and talents. A competent leader will learn how to channel those abilities toward the achievement of a common objective. Ben Carson is a Republican presidential candidate.

- Time is neutral and does not affect the outcome of events. Leaders have the ability to make things happen via their boldness and initiative. A leader's responsibility is to move his or her people from where they are to a place they have never been before. - Jesse Jackson - Henry Kissinger

- **"LEADERSHIP IMPLIES DUTY, HONOR, AND NATION TO ME," SAYS KISSINGER.**

- The feminine traits of leadership, which include aesthetic and environmental awareness, nurturing, affection, intuition, and the attributes that make people feel safe and cared for are all necessary in today's world of fast-paced, technologically advanced life. Deepak Chopra is a well-known spiritual teacher.

- If you think you're capable of more than you think you are, it's because someone else thinks you are. - Zig Ziglar, entrepreneur Innovation distinguishes between those who are leaders and those who are followers. - Steve Jobs

- "Leadership is the skill of providing individuals with a platform on which to propagate ideas that are effective." - Seth Godin.

- Leaders do not create followers; rather, they cultivate more leaders in the organization. - Tom Peters & Associates, Inc. We can't take someone much further than we've gone ourselves, according to John C. Maxwell

- The first and most important responsibility of leadership is to love others. Manipulation is the result of a lack of love in leadership. Rick Warren is a well-known author and motivational speaker.

- Your job is to figure out what you want to do with your life and then to devote your entire being to it. - Buddha's teachings A leader is analogous to a shepherd. He stands behind the flock, allowing the most agile to lead the way, after which the rest of the flock follows, completely unaware that they have been directed from behind the entire time. - Nelson Mandela, in his own words

- Everyone is concerned with changing the world, but no one is concerned with changing themselves. - Author Leo Tolstoy

- When people are hardly aware of a leader's existence, he is at his most effective. When his job is completed and his goal achieved, they will exclaim, "We did it ourselves." - Lao Tzu,

- The Art of War Whatever the human mind can conjure up and believe in, it is capable of achieving. - Napoleon Hill,

- "The Way of the Warrior" We can, we will, and we must work together to achieve our goals. Vice President Joe Biden

- Accept the fact that you will be uncomfortable. Make yourself comfortable with being uncomfortable. It may be difficult at times, but it is a little price to pay for the opportunity to live a dream. - Peter McWilliams & Associates Productivity is enhanced by effective leadership.

- Cultures are built by great leaders. Good leaders provide tangible results. Great leaders help their followers to improve. A clear vision of the future is essential for leaders who want to be successful in their positions. Strong moral character underpins effective leadership. Effective managers serve as role models for their employees in the workplace. Great leaders act as role models for their followers in all parts of their lives, including their personal relationships. - Adam Grant's remark

- There is nothing quite as pointless as working extremely hard to complete a task that should never have been completed in the first place. " - Peter F. Drucker, Jr.

- According to Freud, it is not so much that man is a herd animal as it is that he is a horde animal under the leadership of a chief. - Ernest Becker's etymology

- Pity the leader who finds himself trapped between unloving critics and uncritical lovers. - John Gardner's remark

- An excellent leader inspires people to have faith in him or her and to follow her or him. A strong leader motivates others to believe in their own abilities. First Lady Eleanor Roosevelt

- Leadership is about more than just delivering energy; it is also about unleashing the energy of others. - Paul Polman Polman, Paul
- Average leaders set a high standard for themselves; good leaders set a high standard for others, and exceptional leaders motivate others to increase their own standards. - Orrin Woodward's etymology

- A leader is a dealer in the illusion of success. As Napoleon Bonaparte, the first President of the United States, once said,

- "The ultimate calling of leadership is to enable the growth and development of others." - Harvey S. Firestone & Sons, Inc. is a family-owned and operated business.

- These individuals are carrying out their jobs appropriately and efficiently; those in control of the company are doing the right thing. Leadership, according to Peter F. Drucker Jr., is defined as the ability to transform a vision into a reality.

- As a political activist and author, Ralph Nader contends that the purpose of leadership in today's society is not so much to increase the number of followers as it is to expand the number of leaders. Born in New York City and raised in California, Nader is a writer and activist.

- What industry you work in does not matter; there are several opportunities available. In regions where there is an open mind, it is unavoidable that there will always be a frontier. Theodore Roosevelt, Charles F. Kettering Theodore Roosevelt, Charles F. Kettering.

- Generally speaking, a leader is someone who you will follow to a location that you would not otherwise visit. - The etymology of Joel Barker.

- People are more inclined to believe in a leader than they are to believe in a cause or a concept. Dr. John C. Maxwell, Jr. is an American physician and author.

- Before you can be a leader, you must first focus on developing your own abilities in order to be successful. When you rise to the position of leader, your capacity to develop people will decide your level of success. - A proverb attributed to Jack Welch.

- A leader must first raise his or her own vision to lofty heights, then raise his or her own performance to a higher level, and finally develop one's or her own personality beyond of one's or her own natural restrictions. - Peter F. Drucker, Jr., author of "The Effective Executive".

- It is not difficult to do what is right; it is difficult to do what is right. It is the ability to distinguish between what is correct and what is incorrect. - Lyndon B. Johnson, United States President Neither success nor failures are definitive.

- What matters is the will to keep going no matter what happens. In his book The Battle of Britain, Winston Churchill says: Make sure you do not take the path that could lead you astray. It would be preferable if you could get off the beaten path and leave a trail. A letter to the editor written by Harold R. McAlindon, Jr.

- Keep your fears to yourself, but inspire others by showing your courage in front of them. A conversation between Theodore Roosevelt and Robert Louis Stevenson Effective leadership unlocks people's potential to become better versions of them. Bill Bradley and Associates, Inc.
- To assist those who are performing poorly in improving their performance, and to assist those who are performing well in enhancing their performance even further, is a wonderful leadership goal to pursue. Jim Rohn, a motivational speaker and author, is well-known in the motivational industry.

- Your own personal example is the most potent leadership tool you can use to motivate and inspire those around you. - John Wooden, former UCLA head coach

- A pessimist is someone who is unsatisfied with the direction in which the wind is blowing at the time. The optimist believes that the future will be better than the present. The sails are adjusted by the boat's navigator/leader. Professor John Maxwell, Ph.D.

- For guys who want to do everything alone and claim complete ownership of their successes, it is impossible to be good leaders. The telephone was invented by Andrew Carnegie, who is credited with its invention. However, the leader must be able to communicate effectively in both the visionary and the idealist languages. - A comment made by Eric Hoffer Leaders ponders and discuss various alternatives that might be available. The issues are discussed and contested by the people that are listening in. Brian Tracy is credited with the following quotation: In order to be the conductor of the orchestra, a guy must turn his back on the audience and face forward. - A comment made by Max Lucado Management is about making plans and delegating authority to others.
- Relationships are important in leadership because they allow you to foster and enhance them. To learn more about Tom Peters & Associates, Inc. click here.

- You should never issue an order that cannot be fulfilled. As General Douglas MacArthur put it in his famous quote, "No one is good enough to rule another person without the consent of that other person." - Abraham Lincoln, United States President

- When compared to what you say, what you do has a significantly greater influence on others. - Stephen Covey, "The 7 Habits of Highly Effective People.

- Leadership is about having a vision and accepting responsibility, not about having a lot of authority. - Seth Berkley & Associates, Inc. Seth Berkley & Associates, Inc.

- The ability to recognize a problem before it escalates to the point of becoming an emergency is a significant indicator of leadership ability and effectiveness. - Arnold Glasow & Associates, Inc. - Arnold Glasow & Associates, Inc.

- An excellent leader is one who instills in other men the belief and determination to carry on in his or her own right. Walter Lippman is credited with inventing the term "hypertextual euphemism." In order to motivate others, the best leaders must first bring them together around a single goal. Ken Blanchard is a motivational speaker and author who have written several books.

- A leader is someone who understands the road, has traveled the route, and is demonstrating the way forward in front of others. Dr. John C. Maxwell, Jr. is an American physician and author.

- I am, on the other hand, able to modify my sails in order to always arrive at my destination, regardless of the direction of the wind. - A proverb attributed to Jimmy Dean
- Despite the fact that perfection is impossible to obtain, we can achieve greatness if we work hard and persistently towards it. The famous football coach Vince Lombardi said it best.

- In a situation where there isn't much laughter, there isn't much opportunity for achievement. The telephone was invented by Andrew Carnegie, who is credited with its invention.

- It's ten percent of what occurs to me and ninety percent of how I respond to it that defines my life. This is something I believe to be true. - Charles Swindoll & Associates, Inc. - Charles Swindoll & Associates, Inc.

- Instead of looking for fault, search for a way to solve the problem. - A proverb attributed to Henry Ford Rather than wanting to be successful, strive to be of service to others instead. - Albert Einstein's aphorism about the importance of mathematics in everyday life.

- Even though people will forget what you said and what you did, they will never forget how you made them feel as a result of your actions. This is something I've come to realize. - Maya Angelou, author.

- "I have no qualms about being myself." The mediocre instructor expresses his or her opinions. An excellent instructor will take the time to explain everything. A good example is provided by the excellent educator. An excellent instructor instills confidence in the students. - William Arthur Ward (the poet who wrote the poem).

- It is not the fruit that you reap that should be judged, but rather the seeds that you plant that should be judged each day. "A person who never makes a mistake never attempts anything new," said Robert Louis Stevenson. - Albert Einstein's aphorism about the importance of mathematics in everyday life.

- Maintain your perspective on the fact that not having what you seek might occasionally turn out to be a huge stroke of good fortune for you. His Divine Majesty's honor Tibetan spiritual leader His Holiness the Dalai Lama. Take responsibility for your actions and the people you are in charge of. Grace Murray Hopper said the following.

www.ingramcontent.com/pod-product-compliance
Lightning Source LLC
Chambersburg PA
CBHW070116230526
45472CB00004B/1292